The Canadian Experience
of Public Sector Management
Reform (1995–2002)

COMMONWEALTH SECRETARIAT

Commonwealth Secretariat
Marlborough House
Pall Mall
London SW1Y 5HX
United Kingdom

Published by the Commonwealth Secretariat
Designed by Wayzgoose
Printed by The Charlesworth Group, Huddersfield, UK.

Wherever possible, the Commonwealth Secretariat uses paper
sourced from sustainable forests or from sources that minimise
a destructive impact on the environment.

Price £10.95
ISBN: 0-85092-698 X

Website:
http//www.thecommonwealth.org

Contents

Foreword to the Country Profiles series

Since the successful launch of the Commonwealth Profiles series in 1995, much has happened. When the Auckland CHOGM of 1995 mandated its 'Towards a New Public Administration' Program, many Commonwealth member countries, to a greater or lesser degree, were contemplating or already applying the principles of the New Public Management (NPM) in their civil services. Since that time, the literature on the NPM has been burgeoning, the architecture of civil service delivery has altered dramatically and the debate about the relative success or failure of the NPM continues. In practical terms, the civil services described in the *Profile* series back in 1995 are now often radically different from the scope, organisation and approach of the same civil services today.

The Governance and Institutional Development Division (GIDD) has decided that it is timely to revise and re-issue an updated Profiles Series which attempts both to describe and explain the often tumultuous and controversial public sector reforms of the last seven years as they have unfolded in the contributing countries.

We want these updated Profiles to continue to be a readable, accessible and valuable series, especially for practising bureaucrats, and to serve as reference points for diplomatic, bilateral and multilateral, and political and academic audiences.

Tendai Bare
Director,
Governance and Institutional
Development Division

Dr Peter Frost
Special Adviser,
Public Sector Reform,
Governance and Institutional
Development Division

Preface to the Second Edition

In 1994, Canada produced its first national public sector profile for the Commonwealth Secretariat, but since that time major public sector reforms have continued to take place in Canada. The purpose of this update is to inform the reader about the major reforms that have continued to take place in Canada between 1995 and roughly the end of 2002. Reform has indeed been continuous and it has covered virtually all aspects of public sector management. As a result of this continuous effort to innovate and improve, Canada continues to be seen as a leading example of excellence in public administration and a distinctive Canadian approach has begun to emerge.

The determining factors which created pressure for reform have been very similar to those in many other countries: a financial crisis posing a potential threat to Canada's status as a developed country; the impact of growing globalisation; the rapid development of information technology; and the increasing demands of better-informed citizens.

As a result, some key challenges quickly became obvious: the need to eliminate the deficit; how to change the role of government and get government right; the need to overhaul service delivery; how to engage citizens in the development of policies, programmes and services; the need to reduce and restructure the public service workforce and make effective use of information technology. Efforts to come to terms with these challenges are described in this volume under initiatives such as Program Review, *La Relève*, Citizens First, Government On-Line, Modern Comptrollership and Human Resource Modernisation. Other important sectors where modernisation was needed were those of values and ethics, official languages and diversity. Finally, in recognition of the knowledge-based transformation of our societies and workplaces, increased emphasis was devoted to the development of a continuous learning policy and of learning organisations in the public sector.

One of the Clerks of the Privy Council during this period, Jocelyne

Bourgon, who is now the President of CAPAM (Commonwealth Association for Public Administration and Management), described the Canadian journey as follows:

> *Over a short period of time, Canada managed the most profound realignment of the role of the state since the Second World War. We eliminated the deficit over three years; downsized the scale of the Public Service of Canada as a percentage of GDP to its lowest level since 1949 over five years; modernized our service-delivery function by using modern information technologies and information management . . . a process that is ongoing; as we strengthened our policy capacity; and started to modernize our approach to human resources management.*
>
> *More important, in my view, is the fact that all the reforms were implemented peacefully, without the social unrest and dislocation experienced in other parts of the world. Through it all, the Government of Canada continued to enjoy strong public support.*

She then identified five main characteristics of the Canadian approach to public service reform:

- Firstly, it 'recognised the importance of affordable government but rejected the philosophy that less government is synonymous with better government';

- Secondly, it 'recognised the importance of partnership and strategic alliances';

- Thirdly, it 'reaffirms the importance of citizens well beyond their role as consumers or clients';

- Fourthly, it 'gave equal weight to strengthening policy capacity and modernising service delivery';

- Finally, it 'relied on shared leadership between elected and appointed officials'.

In Jocelyne Bourgon's opinion, these five characteristics

> *... explain, to a large extent, the success of the reform agenda in Canada in the 1990s. Taken together, they also define a distinctive Canadian approach when compared to what was happening in other countries at the same time – and in particular in the United Kingdom, Australia and New Zealand, to name a few.*[1]

1 Speech by Jocelyne Bourgon, President, CCMD, 'The Public Sector in the Knowledge Age – The Canadian Experience: Challenges and Opportunities', CCMD Conference on Changing Governance and Public Sector Reform in the Americas, Ottawa, 2 May 2001.

Like the first edition, this profile only covers the federal public service. Given the federal nature of our country, much reform and innovation also of course occurs at the sub-national or provincial level. The reader is strongly encouraged to consult the other sources listed in the section on further reading. For example, readers could consult the volume by Bourgault, Demers and Williams on Canadian public administration prepared for the 1997 conference of the International Institute of Administrative Sciences in Quebec City. It offers an overview of the historical origins of Canada's public administration systems and of some of their distinctive features, a presentation of the particularities of the Canadian federal system and several chapters on the provinces. They should also consult the Canada report submitted to the Organisation for Economic Co-operation and Development (OECD) in 2002 and continue to explore the Institute of Public Administration of Canada's website, where one can find descriptions of the annual Innovation Awards submissions and winners during this period.

The focus of this profile is on management reforms in the federal public sector. Following a brief section on the organisation and machinery of government, the profile describes the three business lines of the Treasury Board Secretariat (TBS), the government's management board: human resource modernisation, service improvement (including Government On-Line) and stewardship. To this has been added a new section on the management of the policy-making process similar to those included in country profiles produced after the first Canada profile.

The modest purpose of this profile is to present the major reforms that have occurred between 1995 and 2002 and to capture the state of the art in each area at the beginning of 2003. In order to keep the length of the report within acceptable limits, and given the existence of rich websites, the reader is often referred to them and to the further reading and key documents sections at the end of the report. A brief conclusion points to a possible future agenda for public sector management reform, at least from the perspective of the management board.

Several people have toiled over many months to make this publication possible and each and every one of them deserves to be thanked for their support and contribution. The pivotal role played by the International Relations Office and its International Relations Advisory Committee at the Treasury Board Secretariat deserves special mention.

1 The Canadian Context

1.1 Organisation and Machinery of Government

Canada's system of government is based on the Westminster style of responsible government in which the executive sits as part of the legislature and is accountable to an elected House of Commons or provincial legislature.

The manner in which Canadians govern themselves involves three defining characteristics: a constitutional monarchy, federalism and parliamentary democracy.

Constitutional Monarchy
As Canada is a constitutional monarchy, the executive authority of government is vested in the Crown, and exercised on the advice of the Prime Minister of Canada or provincial Premier and his or her Cabinet. The Crown is personified by Her Majesty Queen Elizabeth II, and represented in Canada by the Governor General, and at provincial level by Lieutenant Governors. Royal Assent is required before federal or provincial legislation becomes law.

Federalism
Canada's ten provinces and three territories comprise a federation that is distinguished by a distribution of powers between the federal Parliament and the legislatures of the provinces.

The *British North America Act, 1867* established the Canadian federation as a new Dominion comprising the provinces of Ontario, Quebec, Nova Scotia and New Brunswick. The Act provided for a distribution of governing powers between the federal and provincial levels of government, determined the make-up and powers of the two houses of the Parliament of Canada and provided for the status of the English and French languages.

Subsequent amendments brought six more provinces (Prince Edward Island, British Columbia, Manitoba, Saskatchewan, Alberta, and Newfoundland and Labrador), and three territories (Yukon, Northwest Territories and Nunavut) into the federation.

The *Constitution Act, 1982* incorporated the *British North America Act, 1867* and provided Canadians with a Canadian Charter of Rights and Freedoms and a formula for amending the constitution. The *Constitution Act, 1982* further delineated the powers of the federal and provincial governments.

Parliamentary Democracy

The third defining characteristic of Canadian governance is parliamentary democracy consisting of the Crown, the Senate and the House of Commons.

Most federal laws, including all bills that involve raising revenue or spending money, are introduced in the House of Commons. Each member of the House of Commons represents one of Canada's 301 constituencies, or ridings. The constitution provides that the mandate of a Parliament can last no longer than five years. In practice, Members of Parliament are chosen in federal elections that usually take place every three or four years.

Almost all candidates in federal and provincial elections represent official political parties, although individuals can stand for election as independent candidates. The party that wins the greatest number of ridings or seats in the House of Commons or provincial legislature usually forms the government. At the federal level, the leader of the party with the most votes is asked by the *Governor General* to form a government and become *Prime Minister*. The party with the second largest number of seats forms the official opposition and its leader becomes the *Leader of the Official Opposition*.

Head of Government vs. Head of State

Within this parliamentary democracy, the powers of Head of State and Head of Government are separate. Under the Canadian constitution, the Governor General represents the Crown in Canada and is appointed by the Queen on the advice of the Prime Minister. The

Governor summons, prorogues and dissolves Parliament on the advice of the Prime Minister, and he or she gives assent to Bills that have been passed in both Houses of Parliament. The Governor General also performs many highly symbolic functions as Head of State.

The Prime Minister heads the federal government and is the leader of the political party that has the support of a majority of elected members in the House of Commons. Assisted by his Cabinet, the Prime Minister is answerable to Parliament for the government's actions and decisions.

The Cabinet and Central Policy-Making
As First Minister, it is the Prime Minister's prerogative to organise Cabinet and Cabinet committee decision-making, establish the agenda for Cabinet business and designate committee chairpersons to act on his or her behalf (see section 5.1 for more details).

Central Agencies of Government
In the exercise of their authority, the Prime Minister and the Cabinet are supported both by line departments and by central agencies. Central agencies play an important role in the successful formulation and implementation of government policies and programmes by overseeing interdepartmental mechanisms of information sharing, consultation and co-ordination. They are expected to provide integrated advice and support to the Prime Minister and the Cabinet on government-wide issues and concerns.

Canada has a unique set of central agencies that play an important role in the operation of government.

Privy Council Office
The primary responsibility of the Privy Council Office (PCO) is to provide public service support to the Prime Minister, to ministers within the Prime Minister's portfolio and to the Cabinet in order to facilitate the smooth and effective operation of the Government of Canada. The PCO is the Prime Minister's department and the Cabinet Secretariat (see Section 5.1 for more details on the PCO and the Prime Minister's Office).

The PCO is staffed by career public servants. It assists the Clerk of the Privy Council Office in providing professional, non-partisan support to the Prime Minister in his or her role as head of the public service on all policy and operational issues.

Treasury Board

The Treasury Board is a Cabinet committee established by law and composed of ministers responsible for the management of government expenditure and human resources in the public service. The Treasury Board Secretariat supports the Treasury Board in these responsibilities.

While the Department of Finance is responsible for establishing general policy on government revenues and expenditures, the Treasury Board oversees the management of the budget and credits. It also plays a co-ordinating role in the preparation of the expenditure budget. According to the *Financial Administration Act*, the Treasury Board can deal with any questions concerning financial management, giving it authority over departmental budgets, expenditures, financial commitments, revenue, accounts, personnel management and all the principles governing the administration of the public service. In sum, the Treasury Board is the employer, expenditure authority and general manager of the public service.

Department of Finance

The Department of Finance also plays a co-ordinating role within the decision-making process. The Minister of Finance is responsible for the government's macroeconomic policy, including tax policy and tax expenditures. It is through the Budget exercise that the Minister of Finance establishes a fiscal framework within which the government's expenditure management system can operate effectively.

Through close collaboration and consultation, the Department of Finance and the Treasury Board Secretariat ensure the cohesion and effectiveness of the decision-making process. These two agencies, through the Privy Council Office, provide the Prime Minister and Cabinet committees with advice on policy, related funding issues and the economic impact of proposals before Cabinet. The Department of Finance, in supporting its minister, maintains a broad socio-economic analytical capacity.

Supporting Material

Privy Council Office. *Roles and Structure of the Privy Council Office* *www.pco-bcp.gc.ca*

Communication Canada. *About your Government* *www.infocan.gc.ca*

2 Managing People

2.1 Modernising Human Resources Management in the Public Service of Canada

The Public Service of Canada has served Canadians well for generations. On a daily basis, public service employees enforce laws and regulations, ensure proper stewardship of resources, advise ministers and provide the programmes and services that Canadians want and need. In fulfilling these, and other critical duties, public service employees play an essential role in preserving and promoting the high standard of living that Canadians share.

Over the past decade, public service leaders have moved forward with the realisation of an ambitious modern management agenda. Exercises like the introduction of modern comptrollership have improved departments' collective stewardship capacity, promoted more intelligent risk management and augmented government-wide decision-making abilities. The implementation of the Government On-Line Initiative is improving service delivery and helping to bring government closer to the citizens it serves. At the broader level, the adoption of the management framework, *Results for Canadians*, has clearly established the touchstone for sound public sector management, emphasising citizen-focus, values, results and responsible spending.

Public service human resources management (HRM) reforms are a critical component of this modern management agenda. At a fundamental level, better HRM is the foundation upon which other management change can be successful. HRM reforms will ensure, for example, that the Canadian Government can attract and retain the expertise it needs to realise the move to on-line service delivery. More effective recruiting procedures will make it easier to put the people the organisation needs in the places they are needed, thereby enhancing the government's ability to deliver on its commitments such as improving transparency and reporting to Parliament. Equally, a strong learning culture will increase capacity in areas such as identifying and prudently managing risk.

The Context for Change

A fundamental shift is occurring throughout government as it moves from a philosophy of traditional, time-limited training to one that is learning based in which employees at all levels continually increase their capacity to produce results. Greater emphasis is being placed on expanding employee competencies to ensure a proficient and professional workforce able to meet client expectations.

Human resources management in the Public Service of Canada has evolved over the years as a result of several rounds of reform. In 1918, a three-member Civil Service Commission was established and made responsible for protecting a public service based on merit through functions of recruitment, organisation, classification, compensation, promotion and transfers of personnel. The next significant reforms were in 1961 and 1967 with the update of the *Civil Service Act*, leading to the adoption of the following:

- The *Public Service Employment Act* (PSEA), which governs appointments to the public service, and grants authority over staffing to the Public Service Commission;

- The *Public Service Staff Relations Act* (PSSRA), which introduced collective bargaining;

- Amendments to the *Financial Administration Act* (FAA) which designated the Treasury Board as the employer of the Public Service of Canada.

In the 1990s, *Public Service 2000* led to some changes in the *Public Service Employment Act* designed to increase the powers of deputy ministers and managers. Later in the 1990s, *La Relève* introduced changes to succession planning and new corporate development programmes focusing on senior-level managers. Several new separate employers were established, operating outside the HRM structure of the core public service, among them the Canada Customs and Revenue Agency (CCRA), the Parks Canada Agency (PCA) and the Canadian Food Inspection Agency (CFIA), resulting in greater diversity in HRM in the federal government.

Numerous reports in recent years dealing with public service management have noted the need for clarity in roles and responsibilities, and the need for managers to have greater responsibility and accountability for HRM. Calls for reform of the HRM regime have come from: *Glassco* (Royal Commission on Government Organisation, 1962), *Lambert* (Royal Commission on Financial Management and Accountability, 1979), *D'Avignon* (Special Committee on the Review of Personnel Management and the Merit Principle, 1979), *Public Service 2000* (1990), *Hynna* (Consultative Review of Staffing, 1996), *La Relève: A Commitment to Action* (1997), and the Public Service Commission (*Directional Statement*, 1999).

The statutory elements of the current framework are as follows:

Public Service Employment Act – assigns authority to the Public Service Commission for appointment to and within the core public service, but permits the delegation of staffing authority to deputy ministers. Deputy ministers have statutory authority for deployments (lateral transfers).

Public Service Staff Relations Act – grants the right to collective bargaining. It provides the framework for collective bargaining, and defines and determines the rights and obligations of the employer, employees and bargaining agents. It also provides dispute settlement mechanisms. The PSSRA gives the Public Service Staff Relations Board (PSSRB) the authority to oversee the collective bargaining system and to adjudicate certain grievances. The PSSRB may determine bargaining units and certify bargaining agents as the exclusive representatives of the employees in those units. The PSSRB is an administrative tribunal whose members are appointed by the Governor in Council. Decisions of the PSSRB are subject to review by the Federal Court.

Financial Administration Act – provides for the financial administration of the Government of Canada, the establishment and maintenance of the accounts of Canada and the control of Crown Corporations. Subsection 7(1) of the FAA provides, in part, as follows:

> *The Treasury Board may act for the Queen's Privy Council for Canada on all matters relating to ... (e) personnel management in the Public Service of Canada, including the determination of the terms and conditions of employment of persons employed therein.*

Implementing Change

Canada's ability to compete successfully in the global economy depends on the quality of its public services and the competence and professionalism of public service employees. Innovation, excellence and adaptability in a dynamic federal public service are key to serving Canadians in the new knowledge economy. Among the challenges facing the Government of Canada is the need to attract new recruits into the public service while there is increasing competition for talent in the Canadian labour market.

The Government of Canada is committed to modernising its HRM framework. The existing system was developed more than 35 years ago, based on notions about the workplace that are not consistent with today's workplace culture and the knowledge age. A number of improvements have been made in recent years. Exercises such as *La Relève*, for example, represented an important step in strengthening the development of our future leaders in the aftermath of mid-1990s downsizing. Equally, the Public Service of Canada has made progress in areas such as labour relations, promoting a more culturally and ethnically diverse workplace and creating a more effective and fair executive compensation regime.

However, despite these many and varied improvements, there is a clear and pressing need for more fundamental change. The current legislative and institutional frameworks no longer allow the public service to be as responsive as it must be if it is to continue to serve Canadians. To meet the challenges of the twenty-first century, the Public Service of Canada must transform itself into a modern people-centred organisation, which is more flexible, responsive, adaptive and innovative.

The Rt. Hon. Jean Chrétien, Prime Minister of Canada, announced the formation of the Task Force on Modernising Human Resources Management in the Public Service on 3 April 2001. The task force is mandated to recommend a modern HRM policy, and a legislative and institutional framework which will enable the Public Service of Canada to attract, develop and retain the talent needed to serve the government and Canadians in the twenty-first century.

The task force is reviewing three major interrelated pieces of legislation: the *Public Service Employment Act*, the *Public Service Staff Relations Act* and relevant sections of the *Financial Administration Act*. It is looking at setting the broad framework for the Public Service of

Canada under new legislation that is values based and less prescriptive. In doing so, the task force is guided by three principles:

- Protection of merit through the maintenance of a representative public service that is also people-oriented, non-partisan and competence-based;

- Responsibility for the management of human resources should, to the greatest extent possible, be assigned to managers, be clearly allocated and be pushed down in each organisation as far as possible for the purpose intended;

- All those who share in the responsibility for the HRM of the public service are to be held accountable.

After consulting broadly and examining various options, the task force has crafted a balanced set of proposals for updating the PSEA, the PSSRA and the human resources management provisions of the FAA, as well as the *Canadian Centre for Management Development Act*. The legislation needed to bring these proposals into effect was tabled by the President of the Treasury Board, the Hon. Lucienne Robillard, in Parliament on 6 February 2003. It received House of Commons approval in June 2003 and will be discussed before the Senate in the autumn of 2003.

The Government of Canada is also proceeding with the implementation of several improvements to its HRM regime that do not require legislative changes in support of the work of the task force. These improvements are designed to enhance the ability of executives and managers to manage their human resources more effectively.

Supporting Material

Prime Minister's Office. Press Release: Prime Minister Announces Formation of Task Force on Modernising Human Resources Management in the Public Service, April 2001.
http://www.pm.gc.ca/default.asp?Language=E&Page=newsroom&Sub=newsreleases&Doc=managmenttaskforce.20010403_e.htm

The Treasury Board of Canada Secretariat
http://www.tbs-sct.gc.ca/

The *Public Service Commission of Canada*
http://www.psc-cfp.gc.ca/

The *Public Service Employment Act* (PSEA)
http://laws.justice.gc.ca/en/P-33/

The *Public Service Staff Relations Act* (PSSRA)
http://laws.justice.gc.ca/en/P-35/

The *Financial Administration Act* (FAA)
http://laws.justice.gc.ca/en/F-11/

2.2 Staffing the Public Service – the Public Service Commission

The Public Service Commission (PSC) is an independent parliamentary agency mandated under the *Public Service Employment Act* to uphold the application of merit through the public service staffing system and to safeguard the values of a professional public service – competence, non-partisanship and representation.

The PSC carries out its mission by administering the PSEA and a merit-based system and, *inter alia*, being responsible for the appointment of qualified persons to and within the public service; by providing recourse and review in matters under the PSEA; by delivering training and development programmes; and by carrying out other responsibilities as provided for in the PSEA and the *Employment Equity Act* (EEA).

The PSC has direct authority for recruitment, selection assessment and career counselling of members of the Executive Group. It is also responsible for certain programmes and services on behalf of the Treasury Board, such as development programmes for executives and feeder groups. These programmes include the Career Assignment Program, the Interchange Canada Program, the International Assignments Program, the International Exchange Program, the Business/Government Executive Exchange Program and the Employment Equity Initiatives Program.

All other personnel matters, such as job classification, staff relations and compensation are the responsibility of the employer – the Treasury Board of Canada. The Treasury Board may, in the exercise of its responsibilities in relation to personnel management, including its responsibilities in relation to employer and employee relations in the public service:

(a)   determine the requirements of the public service with respect to human resources and provide for the allocation and effective utilisation of human resources within the public service;

(b)   determine requirements for the training and development of personnel in the public service and fix the terms on which such training and development may be carried out.

The Context for Change

Merit has been the basis of staffing within the Public Service of Canada since 1908. Over time, layers of rules and processes, resulting in a staffing process seen to be slow, cumbersome and unresponsive, obscured this fundamental value.

In recent years, a number of initiatives have been undertaken to modernise the management of people in the public service. In the early 1990s, the Consultative Review of Staffing brought together federal departments, bargaining agents, external stakeholders and the PSC to review and propose a new model for staffing in the federal public service. A move away from a rules-based approach to a values-based approach has emerged as a result.

These reforms have fundamentally reoriented the system by delegating direct staffing authority from the PSC to federal departments and agencies, with the PSC focusing on a proactive oversight role. This evolution is in keeping with the thrust of policy administration elsewhere in the public service that has featured a shift from emphasis on central control to decentralisation with accountability safeguards.

Implementing Change

The PSC's Values-Based Merit Framework is the result of extensive research and consultation with all stakeholders in the staffing system over a period of five years.

Reflecting its legislated mandate to protect the merit principle, and drawing on the work of the Task Force on Public Service Values and Ethics and the Consultative Review of Staffing, the PSC has identified three *results values* – competence, representativeness and non-partisanship; three *process values* – fairness, equity and transparency; and two *management principles* – flexibility and affordability/efficiency that comprise a values-based approach to staffing. These essential components of the framework are presented and defined in Figure 1.

Figure 1: Merit Values and Management Principles

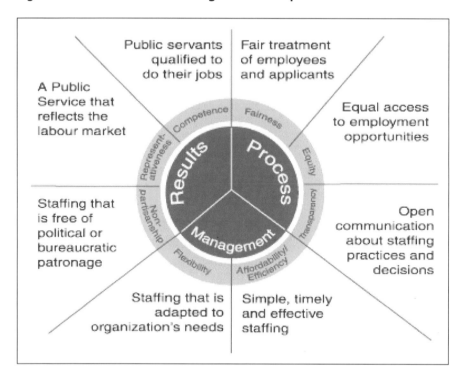

As the PSC delegates more of its powers and moves out of staffing-related transactions, it is focusing increasingly on fostering accountability for merit on a systemic basis. To support this requirement, a modernised accountability infrastructure has been developed. This includes support and guidance to departments and agencies through research and analysis, framework policy approaches to staffing, sharing of best practices and learning tools, and help with tailoring staffing programmes to departmental needs.

This accountability process is supported by a modern approach to oversight that focuses on the overall health of the staffing system and looks at results beyond processes and traditional controls. This oversight is based first on values and management principles and is intended to ensure that all stakeholders are engaged in the Values-Based Merit Framework and to maintain an overview of the staffing system's performance.

The credibility of the delegated staffing system also rests on the effectiveness of the recourse process for those individuals who feel they have not received fair treatment in a particular process. The PSC has modernised the recourse function to integrate staffing values and improve timeliness of decisions, through such measures as a single window for all appeals and requests for investigations. The PSC has also worked with staffing officers to emphasise early intervention and alternative dispute resolution, and has increased the emphasis on systematic learning from experiences related to recourse.

Supporting Material

The Public Service Commission of Canada
http://www.psc-cfp.gc.ca/index_e.htm

Public Service Employment Act
http://laws.justice.gc.ca/en/P-33/

Public Service Employment Regulations
http://www.psc-cfp.gc.ca/staf_dot/pser-refp/pser_e.htm

2.3 Classification Reform

The classification of work is fundamental to any human resources management system. In large and complex organisations, both public and private, it provides a means of grouping similar types of work together so that they can be ranked by levels of difficulty and differentiated from other, dissimilar work. Alignment of the work and the skills required to perform it is essential for the effective recruitment, selection, retention and professional development of employees.

The present classification system was created in the late 1960s to coincide with the introduction of collective bargaining. Public service work was classified and evaluated against a set of classification standards, one for each occupational group. As the years passed, some standards were amended to reflect changes in the work, and new ones were added as new work and new occupational groups emerged, resulting in more than 70 classification standards in use today.

The Context for Change
As with many organisations which have to manage in the new economy, the Government of Canada's system of classifying work has not kept pace with how the work has evolved. Some classification

standards contain outdated notions about public service work. Others describe work that is no longer performed and many exclude important dimensions of current work.

Attempts to reform the public service classification system date back to the mid-1980s. The original design of the Universal Classification Standard (UCS) project, launched in 1997, was to reform the classification system on a universal basis applicable to all occupational groups except the Executive Group. There were two reasons for this plan. First, it was hoped that a common approach to job measurement (one standard versus the current 72) would greatly simplify the system, reduce the administrative burden on managers and lower the administrative overhead costs of maintaining the system. Second, a single classification standard would facilitate the creation of a single corresponding pay structure. The collapsing of all of the occupational group pay structures into one appeared to be the most promising way to ensure compliance with the requirements of the *Canadian Human Rights Act* (CHRA) for equal pay for work of equal value.

Managers, employees and unions across the public service took a fresh look at today's work requirements. This examination uncovered the need to recognise new aspects of work and flagged up where the system needed to eliminate elements that were no longer applicable. New level requirements for some types of work were uncovered and unnecessarily restrictive classification rules were identified for elimination. Work descriptions were updated to better reflect today's operating realities. Departmental managers, unions, employees, classification experts and TBS staff have worked very hard together to modernise and simplify the classification system.

In 2002, the Canadian Government carefully considered a range of perspectives and research to determine the best way to bring the UCS project to maturity. Officials concluded that, although classification reform is necessary to ensure the continued effectiveness of the public service, the universal approach was not workable. This is because applying a single standard and a single pay structure to the more than 150,000 positions in the federal public service would create a management framework that would be too rigid and inflexible for the widely varied work of its employees. As a result, it could impede the government's ability to compete in the marketplace for the talent and skills needed to serve Canadians in the future. Furthermore, it could call into question the role of multiple unions. A new approach was needed.

Implementing Change

On 8 May 2002, the government announced it was adopting a new approach that would allow it to simplify and modernise its classification system in a way that reflects labour market realities, treats men and women equitably, and helps address key government business needs.

The key aspects of the new approach are:

- *Tailored standards.* Classification standards will be tailored to respond to the specific needs of individual occupational groups where existing standards are particularly outdated.

- *Commitment to pay equity.* The Government of Canada is committed to the principle of equal pay for work of equal value in accordance with the *Canadian Human Rights Act.* The TBS supports the Pay Equity Task Force, appointed by the Ministers of Justice and Labour, in its efforts to propose an improved approach to achieving and maintaining equal pay for work of equal value. The TBS is looking forward to the results of its work.

- *A simpler system.* Tailored classification standards will reduce the need for the large number of standards now in use. Progress has also been made in the use of generic work descriptions for similar types of work. These improvements will help reduce the administrative burden and promote employee mobility.

- *A rolling three-year plan.* Implementing classification reform in an organisation as large and varied as the Public Service of Canada will take time. The government will move to a more manageable, multi-year classification reform programme, but this will not happen over-night. This programme will be updated each year and the TBS will monitor efforts and report on its progress and plans annually.

- *Working with departments and agencies and unions.* Classification reform will be carried out in co-operation with departments and agencies, and unions. Based on their feedback, occupational groups may be scheduled for reform or deferred to a later date.

- *Building on past achievements.* The government will build on the updated UCS-style work descriptions that have already been completed to describe employees' positions. It will also work with departments and agencies to ensure that the work descriptions can be used effectively with existing standards for as long as they may be needed.

The new approach to classification reform has several advantages for employees, departments and agencies, for unions and, ultimately, for Canadians. Classification standards can be tailored to the specific requirements of particular occupational groups and priority can be given to those groups in greatest need. Wages can be better aligned to different external labour markets. Unions can continue to negotiate wages for their different memberships in keeping with their diverse and changing needs.

To guide the government's work, several implementation initiatives have been identified and linked into a coherent strategy that groups classification work under three major headings:

- Structural reform of classification standards, that is fundamental change to the basic architecture of standards, tailored to support the business needs of departments and agencies, and conducted on a group by group basis;

- Maintenance of the existing classification standards, where structural reforms have not yet been carried out, or indeed, may not be needed;

- Rebuilding system capacity across departments and agencies.

Significant progress has been made under each heading as the government works towards achieving its initial classification reform milestone, the first formal update to the three-year rolling plan scheduled for May 2003, the anniversary of the President of the Treasury Board's announcement.

Supporting Material

Classification reform
http://www.tbs-sct.gc.ca/classification/

2.4 Ensuring Non-discrimination in Employment Practices

The legislative foundation for ensuring non-discrimination in employment practices is the *Employment Equity Act*. The Act has as its stated objective to:

achieve equality in the workplace so that no persons shall be denied employment opportunities or benefits for reasons unrelated to ability and, in the fulfilment of that goal, to correct the conditions of disadvantage in employment experienced by women, aboriginal peoples, persons with disabilities and members of visible minorities ... .

The Public Service of Canada is covered by this legislation. In addition, there are supporting policies aimed at fostering development of a public service that is representative of the population it serves. Two such policies are the Employment Equity Policy (currently being revised) and the Policy on the Duty to Accommodate Persons with Disabilities in the Federal Public Service that came into effect on 3 June 2002.

The TBS provides policy direction and guidance to federal departments and agencies, monitors and reports to Parliament on the implementation of employment equity, and consults and collaborates with employee representatives (including unions) on implementation measures. The TBS shares employer responsibilities with the Public Service Commission, the agency responsible for staffing in the public service. Several employer obligations, such as conducting a workforce survey, conducting a review of employment systems and preparing employment equity plans, have been delegated to departments and agencies.

The Context for Change

The Government of Canada is committed to employment equity and to the creation of a representative and inclusive workforce. There has been significant progress in implementing employment equity, as evidenced by the increases in representation for all groups designated under the *Employment Equity Act*. Between 1996 and 2001, representation has increased as follows: women from 48.2 per cent to 52.1 per cent; Aboriginal peoples from 2.3 per cent to 3.6 per cent; persons with disabilities from 3.1 per cent to 5.1 per cent; and visible minorities from 4.5 per cent to 6.1 per cent.

However, the employment equity initiative still matters:

• For women, as the public service seeks to increase their representation in executive ranks;

• For Aboriginal peoples, as the public service must address retention issues and a broader distribution of this group among departments and agencies;

- For people with disabilities, as workplace accommodation issues, hiring and career progression need to be addressed;

- For visible minorities, as plans are implemented for increasing the representation of this group overall and in the management ranks of the public service.

Employment equity matters for all as the Public Service of Canada understands and respects differences and seeks to benefit from the contributions of all Canadians.

The *Employment Equity Act* applied to the public service in 1996, making this institution subject to obligations that are similar to those of the federally-regulated private sector. To date, 28 of around 50 federal organisations for which audits have been conducted are in compliance with the legislation.

The current Employment Equity (EE) Policy has as its principal objectives:

- A public service workforce in which Aboriginal peoples, members of visible minority groups, persons with disabilities and women are equitably represented and distributed. Workforce availability and the organisations' operational requirements will be taken into account in determining the equitable representation and distribution of designated groups.

- The identification and removal of barriers in employment systems, policies, procedures, practices, organisational attitudes and established behavioural patterns that have an adverse effect on the employment or career progression of members of designated groups.

- The implementation of special measures to correct the effects of employment disadvantages and promote the workforce participation of designated groups.

- The administration, on behalf of the Treasury Board, of special measure programmes pertaining to designated groups.

Implementing Change

In seeking to address the persistent under-representation of visible minorities in the public service and creating a workplace culture that is more welcoming to diversity, the Government of Canada endorsed in June 2000, the *Embracing Change Action Plan*. This plan established five benchmarks for recruitment, promotion and career development of visible minorities and outlined a series of measures aimed at improving corporate culture and creating a more inclusive work environment.

In June 2002, the Policy on the Duty to Accommodate Persons with Disabilities in the Public Service came into effect to facilitate 'inclusion by design', the creation and maintenance of an inclusive barrier-free work environment. Departments and agencies are currently implementing this policy.

As the largest single employer subject to the *Employment Equity Act*, the Public Service of Canada strives to lead by example. It demonstrates this by being an organisation that embodies fairness, equity and the inclusion of all Canadians. The process of modernising the Public Service of Canada seeks to equip this institution for excellence in service to Canadians in the twenty-first century, and inclusion is clearly a part of such a transformation.

Supporting Material

Employment Equity Act
http://laws.justice.gc.ca/en/e-5.401/text.html

Employment Equity Policy
http://www.tbs-sct.gc.ca/pubs_pol/hrpubs/TB_852/ee_e.asp

Policy on the Duty to Accommodate Persons with Disabilities in the Federal Public Service
http://www.tbs-sct.gc.ca/pubs_pol/hrpubs/TB_852/ppaed_e.asp

Employment Equity in the Public Service, *Annual Report 2000–2001*

Report of the Standing Committee on Human Resources Development and the Status of Persons with Disabilities – Review of the *Employment Equity Act*

Government response to review of the *Employment Equity Act*

2.5 Continuous Learning

Public service employees are called upon each day to deliver programmes and services to Canadians, to advise ministers, to enforce laws and regulations, and to do so with excellence and integrity. In a learning organisation, people at all levels continually strive to improve their capacity to produce results using new ideas, new knowledge and new insights.

The Public Service of Canada is committed to making the most of its knowledge and 'brain power' in order to fulfil its responsibilities in the best way possible. *Life-long learning* is a commitment by individual public service employees to personal and professional development. The ultimate goal is to build a public service *learning organisation* that has two major pillars. The first is the cultivation of an interest in continual growth by individual employees. A learning organisation, however, is not simply an aggregate of individuals who are skilled at learning. It is an organisation that excels at innovative ways of bringing groups of people together in joint inquiry, reflection and discovery. Organisational learning is, therefore, the second pillar, calling on people to work together in mutually beneficial, high-energy collaboration. The new *Policy for Continuous Learning* challenges everyone in the public service to promote the development of a learning organisation. The shared responsibilities require the Treasury Board, as 'employer', to lead a co-ordinated approach to ensure that the individual and organisational learning efforts across the public service produce results that serve the interests of all Canadians.

The Context for Change

The Government of Canada is strongly committed to learning as a key to renewing the public service, strengthening integrity and accountability, supporting innovation and implementing improvements to the management of human resources.

The learning organisation has been a key organising principle since at least 1995. After a wave of fiscal austerity measures, it became apparent that a new 'social contract' was required for public service employees. This movement, known as *La Relève*, ushered in a wide variety of initiatives designed to improve the climate surrounding human resources. By 1999, it was clear that the learning component of *La Relève* needed to be fleshed out further and developed into a broader, more comprehensive framework.

The Committee of Senior Officials (COSO) is a deputy minister committee that provides leadership on issues that affect the entire public service. In support of the *La Relève* movement, and in response to the results of the Public Service Employee Survey of 1999, COSO established the Learning and Development sub-committee. The Learning and Development sub-committee created a list of 44 learning recommendations for action, one of which was the development of a new learning policy for the public service. In the months that followed, many consultations were held with employees, managers, senior learning advisors, bargaining agents, disabled persons and visible minority group members, with federal councils in each region of Canada and with functional communities. The final policy includes input from all of these groups.

The 2002 Speech from the Throne reaffirmed the importance of workplace learning in today's knowledge-based economy, and in May 2002 Treasury Board ministers approved *A Policy for Continuous Learning in the Public Service*. The objective of this policy is to build a learning culture within the public service that stimulates, guides and promotes the public service as a learning organisation committed to lifelong learning for its workforce.

It is worth noting that the second *Public Service Employee Survey*, carried out in 2002, found a significant improvement in both individual and organisational learning. Between 1999 and 2002, all major training and development indicators showed progress: access to training, on-the-job coaching, development of career-enhancing skills, and supervisory and departmental career support. For example, 10 per cent more employees (approximately 16,500 people) received on-the-job training in 2002 than in 1999.

Implementing Change

The continuous learning policy lays the foundation for the public service as a learning organisation. The policy uses a principles-based approach that moves the focus from formal training to continuous learning and fosters individual and collective responsibilities in support of personal and public service-wide learning objectives.

Specifically, the policy states that employees are jointly responsible (with their managers) for their learning plans, should be receptive to learning and should apply their learning to their job. Managers and organisations are responsible for the implementation of the policy and for providing general support to employees.

Departments and agencies are committed to have in place, by 31 March

2004, learning policies, action plans and individual learning plans to support employees' efforts to enhance their professional qualifications, and to create measurable targets and reporting mechanisms on learning.

As the employer, the Treasury Board is committed to developing a learning strategy to address corporate learning needs for the twenty-first century. The strategy will continue to build collaborative union-management relationships in the area of learning; support the development of interdepartmental committees, networks and communities of practice; identify common-knowledge needs of managers and employees and introduce a core package of learning activities to address these needs; develop an orientation programme for all new employees; provide the appropriate financial investment to facilitate the use of e-learning; and evaluate the policy and report on public service results.

A Policy for Continuous Learning in the Public Service recognises that learning is no longer just about training. The policy's approach is in line with a deeper cultural change that is being made as part of management commitment to reform the public service.

The quest to build a learning organisation cannot be considered as one single venture. It is a bundle of loosely connected initiatives, networks and localised activities, all guided by a larger blueprint, infrastructure projects and a set of widely-accessible resources. It is also, by definition, work in progress, since the creation of a learning organisation is a journey. The overarching strategy is guided by the following six broad principles:

1. Learning is not a parallel activity, separate from an organisation's 'mission critical' functions but is, instead, actively aligned with organisational goals. This means that the organisation must create a culture that values learning.

2. Experience is a rich source of insight. Therefore, to build capacity, a public service should reflect on experience, draw valuable lessons from it and share these lessons more broadly.

3. People and diversity are valued. Diversity is a source of strength and learning, as people with different backgrounds and experiences bring new insights to debates.

4. Managers play a crucial role in facilitating learning. Learning must, therefore, play a part in management priorities and activities.

5. A learning organisation is responsible for systematically incorporating citizen input and feedback into organisational practices.

6. A learning organisation systematically reflects on what it does – it evaluates processes and outcomes – in order to continually improve.

Two learning initiatives that are showing particular promise are noted below:

The Joint Learning Program: In autumn 2001, during the collective bargaining process, the Treasury Board Secretariat and the Public Service Alliance of Canada (PSAC), a union that represents a majority of federal public service employees, signed a Memorandum of Understanding to create a Joint Learning Program (JLP) funded at $7 million dollars. The JLP is an innovative initiative and the first learning programme to be negotiated. It offers learning activities for a two-year period to approximately 60,000 union members and to all managers across the country. The overall objective of the programme is to enhance union and management working relationships through learning.

Campus Direct: Campus Direct is a public service-wide e-learning infrastructure initiative that provides public service employees with a 'single window' delivery of on-line courses. It includes a learning portal; a repository of information on learning opportunities and a suite of on-line self-assessment tools; an e-learning library and a host of learning products such as courses; and an e-learning infrastructure and platform to deliver courses and allow managers and learners to keep track of their learning progress.

Supporting Material

Policy for Continuous Learning in the Public Service
http://www.tbs-sct.gc.ca/pubs_pol/hrpubs/tb_856/pclpsc-pacfpc_e.asp

The Joint Learning Program
http://www.jlp-pam.ca/index_e.html

Campus Direct
http://www.campusdirect.gc.ca

2.6 Values and Ethics

This section provides an overview of measures taken concerning ethical conduct in the Public Service of Canada.

Canada has a broad ethics infrastructure allowing it to promote values and ethics in the public service. This infrastructure includes the following legislation and policies: the *Canadian Human Rights Act*; the *Canadian Charter of Rights and Freedoms*; the *Criminal Code* (corruption, fraud and breach of trust); the *Financial Administration Act* (obligations of employees participating in the collection, management and disbursement of public funds, policy against bribes and other matters); the *Official Languages Act*; the *Official Secrets Act*; the *Public Service Employment Act* (oath of office and allegiance, the merit principle and neutrality); the *Conflict of Interest and Post-Employment Code for the Public Service*; the *Government Security Policy* (appropriate use of government information); the *Policy on the Internal Disclosure of Information Concerning Wrongdoing in the Workplace*; the *Policy on the Prevention and Resolution of Harassment in the Workplace*; and the *Policy on Losses of Money and Offences and Other Illegal Acts Against the Crown*.

The basic authority to determine rules governing the conduct of employees in the public service stems from section 11(2)(f) of the *Financial Administration Act* which states that the Treasury Board may 'establish standards of discipline in the public service'. The Act (section 12) enables the Treasury Board to delegate to the deputy head of a department the exercise of its powers and functions in relation to personnel management in the public service.

General principles governing all public service employees are set out in a *Conflict of Interest and Post-Employment Code for the Public Service* (the Code). This policy has been designated by the Treasury Board as a key policy for the management of human resources. In addition, individual departments and agencies have developed their own codes of conduct setting out provisions reflecting the specific nature of their organisations.

The Context for Change
It is government policy to minimise the possibility of conflicts between the private interests and the public service duties of employees, and to resolve any such conflicts in the public interest. The objective is to

enhance public confidence in the integrity of the public service and its employees.

The provisions of the current *Conflict of Interest and Post-Employment Code for Public Office Holders* came into effect on 1 January 1986, and apply to all public service employees for whom the Treasury Board is the employer. All persons appointed to the public service and employees transferred, deployed or appointed to other positions within the public service are required to make a disclosure of any potential conflicts of interest that may exist at the time of their appointment.

Furthermore, under the *Public Service Employment Act*, every deputy head and employee, on appointment from outside the public service, must swear (or affirm) that they will faithfully and honestly fulfil their employment duties and will not, without due authority, disclose or make known any matter that comes to their knowledge by reason of their employment.

Various government bodies have responsibilities under this policy.

The Treasury Board, as the designated authority, will:

- Review and rule on:
  - requests to supplement the compliance measures in the Code;
  - recommendations to designate positions below the executive level as subject to the post-employment compliance measures or to exclude positions from such measures;
  - applications from employees or former employees to reduce the post-employment limitation period specified in the Code;
- Convene panels, as necessary, to advise on the application of the post-employment compliance measures in particular cases.

The Ethics Counsellor (formerly the Assistant Deputy Registrar General) will:

- Provide advice on the most appropriate arrangements required for divestment of assets;
- Serve as trustee of a frozen or retention trust, if requested;
- Assess whether proposals for departmental reimbursement of costs incurred by employees in establishing trusts are appropriate.

The Public Service Commission is responsible for:

- Establishing procedures to ensure that before or upon any appointment, appointees sign a document certifying that they have read and understood the Code and that, as a condition of employment, they will observe it;

- Applying policies and establishing procedures and mechanisms to ensure compliance with the Code regarding Business/Government Executive Exchange and Interchange Canada assignments.

All employees are required to review their obligations under the Code at least once a year. They must take measures to prevent real, potential or apparent conflicts in accordance with the principles of conduct and measures in the *Conflict of Interest and Post-Employment Code for the Public Service*.

The deputy head as designated official must:

- Ensure that employees are informed of the requirements of the Code and that they comply with all its requirements;

- Determine whether real or potential conflicts of interest exist and what action, if any, specific employees have to take;

- Seek Treasury Board approval for any compliance measures that may be required, beyond those the Code specifies, to reflect the department's particular responsibilities or the statutes governing its operations;

- Establish procedures for employees to report official dealings with former public office holders who are or may be governed by the Code's post-employment measures;

- Conduct exit interviews with employees subject to the post-employment compliance measures before they leave the public service or review with employees their responsibility in this regard;

- Ensure that bargaining agents are consulted at departmental level about the administration of the Code, including the implementation of any supplemental compliance measures and the extension of the post-employment requirements to positions other than those in the management category.

The deputy head must request Treasury Board approval on the minister's recommendation to:

- Designate any positions below the level of senior manager as subject to post-employment compliance measures;

- Exclude positions from the application of sections 41 and 42 of the post-employment compliance measures regarding prohibited activities and the limitation period after leaving office.

There are conflict of interests co-ordinators within each government department who provide advice and guidance to managers and employees on potential conflict issues.

Codes are prepared and distributed to assist employees to be aware of their responsibilities with respect to the standards of conduct expected by the department.

Implementing Change

There have been a number of recent developments in Canada with respect to public service ethics and values, and codes of conduct. Two are described below: Comptrollership Modernisation and the *Report of the Task Force on Values and Ethics in the Public Service.*

In 1997, the Independent Review Panel on Modernization of Comptrollership in the Government of Canada tabled its report. In 1998, the pilot phase of modern comptrollership was launched. Three years later, the Treasury Board ministers decided on the government-wide implementation of modern comptrollership.

Modern comptrollership is a management reform focused on the sound management of resources and effective decision-making. It is intended to provide managers with integrated financial and non-financial performance information, a sound approach to risk management, appropriate control systems and a shared set of values and ethics. Every day managers are challenged to make complex decisions. Their behaviour and decisions must be grounded in the values of the public service and of their departments.

The second initiative relates to the *Report of the Task Force on Public Service Values and Ethics.* Under the auspices of the Clerk of the Privy Council and Secretary to Cabinet, a number of deputy minister level task forces were convened in the period 1995–97. One such task force was asked to look at public service ethics and values. The report of the task force concluded that public service ethics and ethical values are evolving; that new ethical challenges are arising from newly emerging values and new circumstances of the public service; and that these may conflict with existing values.

With individual public service employees being asked to exercise more judgement and discretion in programme decisions and decisions on individual cases, and with greater decentralisation and delegation of authority in staffing, contracting and partnerships, employees are concerned about the absence of adequate ethical and accountability frameworks and proper safeguards.

The task force reviewed the current conflict of interest guidelines and post-employment code and found them basically sound but in need of supplementation in at least three ways:

- Guidelines for each department and agency should be tailored to meet its particular challenges and circumstances;

- A more developed central agency capability to counsel individual public service employees and their leaders in matters of ethics and values;

- There was a need for better training and information about existing codes.

Ethical decisions in the new public service environment are often complicated by tensions and shifts in the balance between values, rules and results: for example, emphasis on results versus emphasis on rules and on innovation and risk-taking versus probity and prudence. Further work is required to get this balance right, for example:

- By ensuring that rules are written so that they focus on their substantive purpose and are not overly bureaucratic;

- By enriching the concept of empowering employees by re-emphasising that delegation confers specific and concrete authority to act and thereby implies accountability for specific and concrete results, as well as compliance with rules and procedures;

- By reaffirming the primacy of law, the constitution, regulation and the process as essential pillars of public administration and of the good society;

- By developing a comprehensive ethics regime, including appropriate recourse mechanisms both within departments and agencies and for the public service as a whole.

The task force proposed the elements of an ethics regime:

- A public service code or statement of principles;
- Department and agency-specific codes to adapt and supplement the service-wide code;
- Counselling and recourse mechanisms for public service employees facing a conflict of interest or ethical difficulties.

Ethical values in the public service include integrity, honesty, probity, prudence, impartiality, equity, disinterestedness, discretion and public trust. In many ways these values are no different from ethical values in other parts of society, but what makes them distinctive is their intersection with the democratic and professional values of the public service. Integrity, for example, is required in all professions. Its distinctiveness in the public service lies in the capacity to hold public trust and to put the common good ahead of any private interest or advantage.

The report called for a new moral contract between the public service, the government and the Parliament of Canada. The study team recommended that a government-wide statement of principles be developed, focused on the principles of responsible government, and that it should relate the duties of public service employees to these first principles. Following this, the report called for a series of mutually supportive actions at the service-wide and departmental levels, initiatives that include an interpretation of the statement of principles for the culture and circumstances of each department and agency.

Supporting Material

The Manager's Deskbook, Treasury Board of Canada, third edition

Financial Administration Act
http://laws.justice.gc.ca/en/F-11/

Public Service Employment Act
http://laws.justice.gc.ca/en/P-33/

Treasury Board Manual, Staff Relations Volume (Discipline)

Treasury Board Manual, Human Resources Volume

2.7 Human Resources Planning

Through the Modernising Human Resources Management Initiative (section 2.1), the Public Service of Canada aims to create a capacity for strategic human resources planning that will include a results-based focus with a new emphasis on measurement. In the meantime, the Treasury Board Secretariat, representing the employer, provides information, guidance and support for HR planning throughout the public service.

The Context for Change

The Human Resources Management Framework (HRMF) is a guide developed by the TBS for all managers and human resources practitioners of the Public Service of Canada to help them improve human resources management in their organisations in support of their business objectives. Designed as a practical, desk-side reference tool, it is an essential component of the learning curriculum for middle managers, as it reflects current trends and developments in the field of human resources management. The HRMF also presents an inventory of human resources management practices that have demonstrated a positive impact on business performance, as well as those that are unique to the public service environment. The framework is being updated to bring a results-based management focus to all aspects of human resources management, including planning.

Implementing Change

In order to provide a forum for federal departments and agencies to share their experiences and best practices in HR planning, a *Human Resources Planning Interdepartmental Network* (HRPIN) has been set up. The HRPIN also publishes reports and provides tools for the HR community, such as a *Guide to Strategic Human Resources Planning*.

In addition, the TBS provides annual statistics on the federal public service workforce covering aspects such as its size and composition, the types of employment and the regional distribution of employment equity groups, and mobility data and statistics relating to them. In addition, through the Joint Centre for Demographic Analyses, the PSC and the TBS provide data on public service demographics that enable departmental human resources personnel and managers to improve their planning.

Each department is encouraged to report on the status of its modern management initiatives in its annual Departmental Performance Report (DPR). Human resources management is one of the key management initiatives expected to be covered in the DPR, as it underpins *Results for Canadians: A Management Framework for the Government of Canada.*

Supporting Material

The Human Resources Management Framework: A Reference Tool for Managers
http://www.tbs-sct.gc.ca/hr-rh/hrtr-or/Framework/FRAME_e.asp

Results for Canadians: A Management Framework for the Government of Canada
http://www.tbs-sct.gc.ca/res_can/siglist_e.html

Employment Statistics for the Federal Public Service
http://www.tbs-sct.gc.ca/pubs_pol/hrpubs/pse-fpe/es-se99-00_e.html

2.8 Human Resources Information Systems

Human resources information is all information pertaining to the current and potential human resources population of government agencies and departments, including both current and historical information.

Human resources information systems are operated and maintained within each federal department and agency to support personnel management requirements within each organisation. Fifty-two departments and agencies are members of one of the three endorsed Human Resources Shared Systems clusters. The TBS plays a bridging role between these clusters to minimise diversification and to support the development of additional common capability.

There are also a number of unique human resources systems owned and operated by large departments with in-house information technology organisations and significant investments in technology. By contrast, at the other end of the HR systems and services spectrum, are small departments and agencies with little, or no, in-house capability to support their HR system requirements.

Regardless of size, departments and agencies share one common characteristic – each is a unique stand-alone silo of HR information; all transactions with other departments or with central agencies require significant levels of effort.

Human resources information is centrally collected under the authorities and obligations described in the *Financial Administration Act* and the *Public Service Staff Relations Act* . Pursuant to the general powers described under the FAA and PSSRA, the Treasury Board maintains personnel information systems on public service employees. These data banks are the prime source of information for TBS users to:

- Plan, implement, evaluate and monitor government policies;

- Support human resources planning and management, including collective bargaining compensation analysis, official languages and employment equity;

- Respond to special requests for information and conduct research, special studies and surveys as it relates to employee-related personnel information and Access to Information and Privacy requests;

- Support the development and administration of various insurance and medical plans.

The Context for Change

Human resources management functions are business functions that occur in the planning, administration and control of human resources in the government.

Information management is the planning, directing and controlling of all the organisation's information-based resources to meet corporate goals and to deliver programmes and services. On 3 April 2001, the Prime Minister announced the formation of the Task Force on Modernising Human Resources Management in the Public Service to support the President of the Treasury Board in human resources management reforms within the public service (see section 2.1). The majority of the changes anticipated will require major changes in the roles, responsibilities and accountabilities of the institutions dealing with human resources management in the public service, including the Treasury Board, its Secretariat, the PSC and the Public Service Staff Relations Board.

The legislative proposals being developed by the task force will provide a legal framework for modernisation but many other improvements will come through non-legislative initiatives. The intention of the HR information systems aspects of human resources management modernisation is to eliminate obstacles to inter-operability/integration of government HR systems, to improve the quality and accessibility of HR information repositories and to promote increased migration of departments and agencies to shared HR systems clusters.

Effective HRM ensures that the public service is composed of non-partisan, professional, competent, highly-qualified individuals who are representative of the Canadian population as a whole. At all organisational levels, HRM seeks to deploy these human resources to carry out government policies and to deliver services to the public. Public service employees are recognised as contributors to be valued and developed.

The Canadian Government's human resources information management has the following 18 functional areas:

- HR Utilisation and Planning
- Staff Relations
- Organisation Analysis and Design
- Classification
- Staffing
- Compensation
- Performance Assessment
- Training and Development
- Organisation Development
- Leadership and Supervision
- Incentives and Recognition
- Management of the Executive Group
- Occupational Health and Safety
- Official Languages
- Employment Equity

- Leave

- Workforce Adjustment

- Separation.

Departments and agencies must support the management of their human resources with practical and effective information and supporting systems and processes. A key consideration is to make sure that as much information as possible is created directly by authoritative and affected parties (for example employees or managers), and that human resources information is shared with or transferred to appropriate HR functional areas and to other functional domains in which it has value, such as finance.

In order to implement or improve an HR information system, a number of steps must be followed:

- The need to move beyond processing HR transactions and storing HR information needs to be appreciated;

- The direct requirements of employees and managers must be given a high priority;

- Direct service to employees and managers must be pursued in a manner that reduces dependence on intermediaries;

- The capabilities of current web-based technologies and best-of-breed commercial HR applications must be exploited;

- Government-wide information and technology management standards need to be applied.

Implementing Change

A fundamental step in improving the overall level of service provided by the federal government's HR information systems is to focus the scarce resources in departments and agencies within a small number of applications. To that end, all departments and agencies are strongly encouraged not to invest further in unique, legacy HR information systems, but to transit to an endorsed HR shared system as the need arises. In this way, common business processes can be developed and government resources can be applied in such a way as to benefit more than a single organisation.

Current service-wide human resources information systems are a group of separate information systems that collect and consolidate departmental human resources data. System records vary according to specific system requirements, and contain basic employee and position information.

The following systems make up the current set of the federal government's service-wide human resources information systems:

Employment Equity Target Group Data Bank (EEDB): This data bank is used to identify members of the public service who are Aboriginal, disabled persons and/or members of visible minorities for analysis purposes. It facilitates comparison of their representation in the public service with their presence in the general population. It is also used to analyse and monitor the situation and progress of the survey target populations as compared to the rest of the public service in terms of regional and occupational distribution, training, mobility, etc.

Entitlements and Deductions System (EDS): This system holds individual federal employee data relating to pay and benefits. It includes the reference numbers for various insurance and medical plans and the entitlements and deductions of each individual.

Extra Duty Reporting System (EDRS): Included here are individual federal employee data relating to overtime and extra duty usage. It applies to all current employees for whom the Treasury Board is classed as the employer under the *Public Service Staff Relations Act*, Schedule 1, Part I.

Incumbent System (INC): This system contains individual federal employee data relating to personnel matters. It includes information concerning collective bargaining, exclusions, bargaining agents and languages.

Leave Reporting System (LRS): This information bank houses individual federal employee data relating to paid leave. It applies to all current employees for whom Treasury Board is classed as the employer under the PSSRA, Schedule 1, Part 1.

Leave Without Pay System (LWOP): This system provides information on individual federal employee usage of leave without pay.

Mobility File (MOB): Data are provided on individual federal employees' movement into, within or out of the public service.

Position Exclusion System (PES): This bank provides a record of individual federal employee information relating to exclusions, and applies to all former and currently excluded employees for whom Treasury Board is classed as the employer under the PSSRA.

Position and Classification Information System (PCIS): The system contains individual federal employee data relating to position classification matters. It is used to support the development and administration of the classification system and the Official Languages Program within the public service, in addition to other uses.

Workforce Adjustment Monitoring System (WFAMS): This data bank provides the TBS with information on the Workforce Adjustment cash-outs of employees leaving the public service, under the various Workforce Adjustment policies and programmes. It is used to monitor the implementation and ongoing departmental compliance with the provisions of these various policies and programmes.

Supporting Material

Shared Systems Initiative
http://www.cio-dpi.gc.ca/ssi-isp/index_e.asp

Government On-Line Initiative
http://www.gol-ged.gc.ca/index_e.asp

HR Tools and References
http://www.tbs-sct.gc.ca/hr-rh/hrtr-or/index_e.asp

Information for Federal Employees
http://www.tbs-sct.gc.ca/audience/emp_e.asp

2.9 Advisory Committee on Senior Level Retention and Compensation

In 1997, the then President of the Treasury Board, the Hon. Marcel Massé, established the *Advisory Committee on Senior Level Retention and Compensation*, comprised of senior officials from the broader public and the private sector.

The Advisory Committee's mandate is to provide independent advice and recommendations to the President of the Treasury Board concerning executives, deputy ministers and other Governor-in-council appointees of the federal public service on:

- Developing a long-term strategy for the senior levels of the public service that will support HRM needs;

- Compensation strategies and principles, including rates of pay, rewards and recognition;

- Overall management matters including human resources policies and programmes.

The Context for Change

When the Advisory Committee was established, the public service was emerging from the Program Review exercise, during which many departments and agencies had reduced their staff. There had also been a number of years of restrictions on hiring and no increases in salaries. Research indicated that careers in the public service were not attractive to new university graduates. In addition, demographic projections showed that the public service would be losing a large number of its senior level employees over the coming decade, with a very high proportion of executives eligible to retire within ten years.

It was against this backdrop that the Government of Canada established the Advisory Committee to provide advice and recommendations regarding the challenge of recruiting and retaining the qualified senior-level employees required to ensure the future excellence of the federal public service.

Implementing Change

In the context of a looming demographic crisis and a decade of fundamental change in the public sector, the Advisory Committee concluded that a growing human resources deficit required immediate attention in order to protect the quality of the public service and, inevitably, Canada's economic well-being.

The Committee identified the need for a clear public service vision for the future, the need for cultural and human resources renewal, and compensation as the most pressing concerns requiring urgent attention.

The Advisory Committee highlighted a requirement for new approaches to compensation for the senior levels of the public service. It expressed the view that an organisation's compensation policy should be designed to attract and retain the appropriate calibre of employees to achieve its objectives. The Committee addressed the principles on which compensation should be based and recommended a compensation structure in line with these principles. Recommendations included:

• That the total compensation package for the senior level groups should be distinct from that offered to unionised employees;

• That the cash compensation should consist of two components – a salary structure that has a range for each level with the job rate (range maximum) adjusted at intervals using market comparisons of total compensation in appropriate comparator groups, and a pay-at-risk component tied to achievement of annual objectives;

• That processes be put in place to remove, as far as possible, the year-to-year administration of public service compensation from the political arena.

As a result of the committee's first report, significant elements of senior level compensation were approved by the Treasury Board and implemented. In 1998, a new salary structure aligned salary rates at the lowest executive levels with the private and broader public sectors and improved relative competitiveness at the more senior levels. In 1999, the Treasury Board introduced the Performance Management Program to support a new scheme of variable at-risk compensation paid on the basis of performance measured against agreed objectives and the achievement of business plans. In accordance with the Committee's recommendations, the Performance Management Program was designed to:

• Reflect the values of a public service focused on the public interest;

• Identify objectives that could be individual, team-related or corporate and that would encompass a range of elements, including effective management of resources, leadership linked to quality service, policy advice, innovations and, most importantly, results and exemplification of core values;

• Allow for the review of significant changes during a measurement period and the continual evaluation of performance;

• Be an integral part of total compensation, paid each year on the basis of actual performance against agreed objectives.

Taken together, the revised salary structure and pay-at-risk programme contributed to restoring integrity to the compensation system and improving transparency and competitive standing, and began the process of better aligning rewards and performance.

The committee also recognised that the government could not avoid a serious human resources deficit in the public service simply by improving executive compensation. The first recommendation of the Advisory Committee was in fact to establish a vision and culture for the public service that encompasses a shared understanding of core values and changing roles and responsibilities and a sense of common purpose, all of which would help to inspire and challenge the Canadian public service and strengthen its relationship with those it serves.

In its second and third reports, the committee re-affirmed the key challenges of public service renewal – the need for cultural change, for improved human resources management and for attention to be paid to the nature of the work, as well as the workplace, that the public service can offer. Through its expert advice and recommendations that improved the integrity of the compensation system, and its efforts in highlighting structural and cultural obstacles, the Advisory Committee has helped to lay the groundwork for modernising the human resources management regime for the senior levels of the federal public service.

In June 2001, the President of the Treasury Board, the Hon. Lucienne Robillard, renewed the mandate of the Advisory Committee for a further three years.

The committee's fourth report recapped the progress made under the previous three reports, outlined proposals regarding several outstanding human resources issues and made specific recommendations on compensation aimed at improving the timeliness and the comparability of senior public service compensation with that of the external public and private sectors.

The committee pressed quickly on to publish a fifth report that included recommendations on the human resources issues on which it had made proposals in March 2002. The revised methodology for compensation comparison recommended by the committee allows for more timely input and will permit the committee to make its compensation recommendations early in 2003 and in subsequent years. This enables the committee to focus more of its attention on a broad range of human resources issues affecting the senior levels of the public service as it works with the government in support of an exemplary workplace that will continue to retain and attract qualified employees to serve Canadians.

Supporting Material

Advisory Committee on Senior Level Retention and Compensation –
First Report, January 1998
http://www.tbs-sct.gc.ca/pubs_pol/partners/acslr1_e.asp

Advisory Committee on Senior Level Retention and Compensation,
Second Report, March 2000
http://www.tbs-sct.gc.ca/pubs_pol/partners/ac_15_e.asp

Advisory Committee on Senior Level Retention and Compensation,
Third Report, December 2000
http://www.tbs-sct.gc.ca/pubs_pol/partners/strong/acslr_e.asp

Advisory Committee on Senior Level Retention and Compensation,
Fourth Report, March 2002
http://www.tbs-sct.gc.ca/hr-rh/in-ai/correspondence_files/2002/acslrc-ccmpr-letter_e.asp

Advisory Committee on Senior Level Retention and Compensation,
Fifth Report, August 2002
http://www.tbs-sct.gc.ca/pubs_pol/partners/acslrc-ccmpr-5_e.asp

2.10 Pride and Recognition

It is the policy of the Government of Canada to recognise public service employees for the outstanding performance of their duties, for other meritorious contributions related to their duties, for practical suggestions for improvements, for excellent day-to-day efforts and for dedicated long service.

Public service employees are seen to warrant both formal and informal recognition, and a considerable commitment is being made to implementing effective, flexible and meaningful recognition practices in departments and agencies. The pride and recognition framework aims at creating a workplace where people are valued, recognised and treated in accordance with the core values of the public service. It strives to foster a deep and abiding pride in the work that public service employees undertake.

The Context for Change

In 1987, the Treasury Board approved an employee recognition policy known as the *Incentive Award Plan (IAP)*. The idea of using performance incentives was put forward in December 1990, as part of *Public Service 2000*. As a result of recommendations of the Public Service 2000 Task Force, the government proposed amendments providing greater flexibility to deputy ministers, allowing them to phase out performance pay (only a portion of the reward or bonus is built into the salary base) and replace it with performance rewards, and to delegate authority to departmental managers for the granting of awards. The development of these awards enables departments to use non-monetary recognition vehicles suitable to departmental specific needs.

The Sub-committee of Senior Officials on Pride and Recognition, made up of deputy and associate deputy ministers, was created in March 1997 to develop and implement an action plan to foster pride and promote recognition in the public service. Its mandate fell within the *La Relève* initiative to build a vibrant and modern federal public service for the future. In a context of promoting a public service culture of recognition that could move beyond formal awards programmes, the committee set up a network of departmental and agency Pride and Recognition Champions in 2001–2002.

Before that, early in 1996, the TBS initiated an evaluation of the IAP as part of public service renewal and on 28 May 1998, a new Recognition Policy was put into effect to replace the IAP and to manifest the expressed need for a values-based policy offering departmental managers greater flexibility in employee recognition practices. In support of the *National Public Service Week Act (NPSW)* introduced in 1992, the Recognition Policy also outlined central and departmental responsibilities regarding these important annual celebrations. Increasingly since its inception, NPSW has become a notable and significant event in the pride and recognition calendar.

Implementing Change

More and more, the recognition of employees is being seen as a fundamental and ongoing requirement of sound performance management practice; it is seen as central to the validation of employees' work life experience and to the health of the workplace, having a direct impact on recruitment and retention. The structure and practice of pride and recognition programmes in the federal government are continuously evolving to reflect this philosophy.

Today, the pride and recognition programmes have evolved into an impressive array of tailor-made departmental and agency programmes. These include programme elements ranging from those patterned after the formal aspects of the Recognition Policy to much broader and more spontaneous, i.e. 'instant' and 'day-to-day' practices and initiatives.

The Recognition Policy provides for the following:

Departmental Awards

These are awards that are managed, granted and financed by departments and agencies. They include:

Long Service Awards

Long Service awards, which recognise the faithful service of employees of the Government of Canada, are presented to employees after 15, 25 and 35 years of service, and to employees who are retiring after a minimum of 10 years of service in the federal public service. Some federal organisations recognise additional milestones such as 10, 20, or 30 years of service.

Formal Awards

Formal awards are awards granted to employees who have demonstrated meritorious accomplishments or service in the performance of their duties. Both individuals and groups are eligible. Such awards can consist of various memorabilia, chosen at the discretion of the granting department or agency, which must not exceed the prescribed limits of $5000 for an individual and $10,000 for groups. Suggestion awards, i.e. awards that encourage public service managers and employees to look for new and better ways to increase the efficiency and effectiveness of government operations and service to the public, are considered to be formal awards and are often bestowed by departments and agencies. Employees who are part of a performance pay plan are not eligible for cash awards but may receive non-monetary recognition.

Informal ('Instant') Awards

Departments and agencies may also develop their own special informal awards, designed to recognise and promote public service values, to reinforce the ways people work together in organisations, to encourage teamwork and partnerships, and to promote a client-centred, results-oriented focus. Departmental informal recognition awards are non-monetary, and should not exceed $500 in value for individuals and $1000 for groups.

Corporate Awards

Corporate awards are public service-wide awards managed by the TBS with input in the form of nominations from departments and agencies. Awards include:

Awards of Excellence and Employment Equity and Diversity Awards
Every year, an Awards and Recognition Board selects the most innovative, exemplary or unique contributions from formal departmental award recipients from across the public service and recommends them to the President of the Treasury Board for additional recognition. A specially designed pin, trophy and certificate are presented at a national ceremony during *National Public Service Week*. The Employment Equity and Diversity Award recognises organisations and individuals who, through their ongoing diligence and commitment, are helping the public service become representative and inclusive.

Outstanding Achievement Awards
Outstanding Achievement awards are presented to career public service employees occupying a full-time position in the executive group or at the deputy minister level (or equivalent). The award recognises sustained and outstanding performance in the public service, demonstrating both enlightened leadership and service-oriented innovation. This award consists of a citation signed by the Prime Minister and the Governor General, a gold pin and a Canadian work of art with a maximum value of $10,000.

Head of the Public Service Awards
The Head of the Public Service awards recognise employees who best exemplify the work of public service employees in meeting the challenges outlined in the Clerk of the Privy Council's *Annual Report to the Prime Minister on the Public Service of Canada*. Up to a maximum of 20 awards are granted per year, consisting of a trophy and a certificate signed by the Clerk of the Privy Council.

Emphasis continues to be placed on ensuring that the intent of the programme and the newest developments in the pride and recognition field are communicated to departmental co-ordinators via the national Pride and Recognition Conference, which takes place annually in the environs of the national capital region.

The COSO Sub-committee on Pride and Recognition is carrying on its work and is exploring opportunities to engage departmental Pride and Recognition Champions in their departmental action planning vis-à-vis fashioning an authentic and meaningful recognition culture. In this, a new strategic framework for action is being developed by them which will include communication activities, a treatment of the fundamental question of underlying values, an implementation of managerial and employee recognition training and a tie-in to related and complementary workplace well-being issues.

The 2002 *Public Service Employee Survey* results show an improvement in the degree of pride in their work felt by public service employees since the last survey of 1999 and activities are evolving to continue this pride and recognition paradigm shift. Recognition programmes are an integral part of quality performance management, of continued performance improvement and of workplace validation.

Supporting Material

Bravo!, COSO Sub-Committee on Pride and Recognition and Public Works and Government Services Canada, 2001

The Manager's Deskbook, Treasury Board of Canada, third edition

Treasury Board Manual, Human Resources Volume, chapters 1–6

Public Service 2000: The Renewal of the Public Service of Canada, The Government of Canada, 1990

2.11 The Public Service Employee Survey

This section deals with the innovative introduction of public service-wide surveys of employees in the late 1990s.

The Context for Change

Why was this conducted?
In 1997, based on three principal public service initiatives (*La Relève*, Human Resources Management Framework and Modern Comptroller-ship), the Clerk of the Privy Council introduced the idea of a voluntary survey of all federal public service employees (those who are identified in Schedule 1, Part 1 of the Public Service Staff Relations Act and for whom the Treasury Board of Canada is the employer).

This decision was taken due to challenges (restructuring and reorganisation, programme and priority changes, compensation freezes and downsizing) that the public service had undergone in the past few years. Many public service employees had been personally and professionally affected by these changes. Moreover, survey feedback was recognised as a cornerstone of progressive organisations seeking to improve well-being and service to clients.

The Treasury Board Secretariat was tasked with implementing the project. The TBS worked in consultation with other key federal departments and agencies to develop a survey that would gather information from all employees through a common questionnaire. In October 1998, the Committee of Senior Officials endorsed the project. It was agreed that the survey would be conducted in the spring of 1999.

By using one instrument at a common point in time, the survey provided the first comprehensive and consistent 'snapshot' of employees' workplaces, addressing such issues as diversity, career aspirations, learning and developmental needs.

Implementing Change

How was it conducted and what were the results?
This was the first time that a survey of this nature was conducted, and the first time that the Government of Canada was able to see how the views of employees in departments or agencies related to the views of other employees across the public service.

Questions were chosen based on what research showed to be important in developing and maintaining high-performing organisations. A variety of other long-standing and rigorously developed standards and frameworks of good organisational performance were used, including the Investors in People model (England), the National Quality Institute standards (Canada) and field research conducted among large corporations in Canada and the USA. The questions were developed in consultation with a number of departments and agencies and pre-tested with employees in focus groups held across Canada.

Statistics Canada administered the survey on behalf of the TBS. In accordance with the *Statistics Act*, Statistics Canada guarantees that individual respondents will not be identified in any way. Employees received a copy of the survey questionnaire with their 24 May 1999 pay cheque or pay stub. A stamped, self-addressed envelope was included with the survey. Once completed, the questionnaires were returned to Statistics Canada.

Over 190,000 questionnaires were distributed to public service employees in Canada and abroad. Of these, more than 104,000 responded, which represents a response rate of 55 per cent. As the demographic profile of those who responded matches that of the public service as a whole, the results represented a good basis for analysis.

After preliminary analysis, the results of the survey indicated that although employees felt that their work was important, were proud of their work, liked their jobs and thought their organisation was a good place to work, there were areas where improvement was needed. The following concerns were identified: a call for more management support to employees, as well as a need to address suggestions of harassment and discrimination in the workplace; a need to improve workplace well-being (pride, recognition, workload, coaching, classification, staffing); and a need to address career development and learning.

On 10 November 1999, the TBS disseminated the public service-wide results and a summary report using the survey internet site and printed materials. In addition to the website and the printed copy, the public service-wide results were made available in Braille, audiocassette, large print and diskette. On 18 November 1999, the TBS disseminated departmental and agency results using the survey website. It was at the department's discretion to determine the format of the release. Departments and agencies were also encouraged to produce a summary report to their employees.

What have the results been used for? What has changed?
The results of the survey provided a good baseline to help in efforts to improve the workplace and deliver better services to Canadians. Since the findings of the survey results, many workplace initiatives have occurred, and actions have been taken both by central agencies and line departments and agencies to address the issues identified in the survey. Descriptions of some workplace improvement initiatives are available via the survey website.

Second Public Service Employee Survey
In early spring of 2001, it was decided that the TBS would conduct a second survey to help measure progress since the first Public Service

Employee Survey. As in 1999, Statistics Canada administered the survey on behalf of the TBS.

The questions for the second survey were chosen based on their usefulness to employees, managers and bargaining agents in helping to identify issues and provide concrete solutions to improve the workplace and service to Canadians. The questionnaire was developed by an Inter-departmental/Union Survey Working Group composed of representatives from small, medium and large departments and agencies, Statistics Canada, central agencies, bargaining agents and external advisors.

The second survey explored the same themes as the 1999 Survey, including harassment and discrimination, workload, career development, communications, leadership, service to clients and staffing. Over 50 per cent of the questions from the 1999 Survey were repeated. A number of other questions were revised and expanded for greater clarity and to obtain more meaningful data in areas such as harassment and discrimination, well-being and work-life balance, career development and fairness in the staffing process.

New themes were also introduced to explore other areas of workplace concern, such as official languages, health and safety, values and ethics, retention and labour management relations.

The survey period ran from 22 May to 21 June 2002. The questionnaire was provided to employees in a 'paper copy format' only. Once completed, questionnaires were returned directly to Statistics Canada. Statistics Canada accepted completed questionnaires for several weeks following the established survey period.

A survey questionnaire was distributed to all employees in departments and agencies listed under Schedule 1, Part 1 of the *Public Service Staff Relations Act* (PSSRA 1-1) for which the Treasury Board represents the employer. Employees meeting the following status were eligible to participate in the 2002 Survey:

Indeterminate employees (permanent)
Seasonal employees
Employees on assignment
Term employees
Casual employees

Over 165,000 questionnaires were distributed to employees in Canada and abroad. More than 95,000 employees responded. The response rate was up from 54.6 per cent in 1999 to 57.8 per cent. This provided a solid basis for analysis and comparison with the 1999 Survey.

The survey results indicated improvement in several areas since the 1999 Survey. Of the 39 questions or sub-questions that were repeated verbatim (excluding questions on general information), improvement was seen in 34 areas. Although there has been an increase in employee satisfaction, there is still work to do in areas such as harassment and discrimination, career and learning, workload/work-life balance, leadership and labour management relations.

On 2 December 2002, the TBS disseminated the public service-wide results and a summary report via the survey website. In addition, a paper copy of the public service-wide report was sent to all employees and copies were made available in Braille, audiocassette, large print and diskette upon request.

On 9 December 2002, all departments and agencies released their departmental and organisational unit results to their employees via departmental intranet or print format. It was at the discretion of departments and agencies to determine the format of the release. Departments and agencies were also encouraged to produce a summary report for their employees. The TBS posted departmental results on the survey website on 9 December 2002.

Survey Follow-up

A Survey Follow-up Action Advisory Committee (SFAAC) has been established. The committee is comprised of representatives from the TBS, departments and agencies, managers' communities, unions and outside experts. The TBS chairs the committee and provides secretariat services.

The committee will recommend through the Chair of the SFAAC to deputy ministers, heads of agencies and other key stakeholders, reasonable, do-able initiatives that respond to the second Public Service Employee Survey in the short, medium and long term. The SFAAC report will address four or five public service-wide issues for potential action with defined accountabilities and identify clear goals, such as policy review, including recommendations on how this work could be conducted and by whom. A Technical Analysis Advisory Committee has also been formed and is composed of central agency representatives and Statistics Canada. This team will provide in depth analysis of survey results and will support the SFAAC. A Policy Analysis Group has also been formed to address in detail the potential impact of the survey results on public service policy.

Supporting Material

Supporting Material is available via the survey website at the following address:
http://www.survey.sondage.gc.ca

2.12 Health and Safety in the Workplace

The objectives of the government's Occupational Health and Safety Policy are to promote a safe and healthy workplace for public service employees and to reduce the incidence of occupational injuries and illnesses. This policy applies to departments and agencies listed in Schedule 1, Part 1 of the *Public Service Staff Relations Act*.

The Context for Change

The part of the public service for which the Treasury Board is the employer became subject to the provisions of the *Canada Labour Code*, Part II and its pursuant regulations in 1986. Part II of the code governs occupational health and safety in the workplace and, more specifically, is intended to prevent accidents and injury to health arising out of, linked with or occurring in the course of employment. Three fundamental rights of workers underlie the legislation:

- The right to know about known or foreseeable hazards in the workplace;

- The right to participate in identifying and resolving job-related safety and health problems;

- The right to refuse dangerous work if the employee has reasonable cause to believe that a situation constitutes a danger to him/herself or to another employee.

In 1993, representatives of the TBS, other major employers and labour organisations began an intensive consultation process with a view to improving occupational health and safety in workplaces under federal jurisdiction. New legislation came into effect on 30 September 2000.

Implementing Change

The new legislation gave employers and employees expanded responsibilities to ensure a healthier and safer work environment. The amendments were intended to foster an environment that allows these parties to assume greater responsibility for their own workplace regulation by giving them the discretion to identify and resolve health and safety hazards as they arise.

Organisations with 300 or more employees must establish a Health and Safety Policy Committee, with equal representation from managers and employees. The committees are involved in the development of occupational health and safety related prevention programmes, investigations, studies and inspections, and the assessment of personal protective equipment. The establishment of these committees at the corporate level ensures that health and safety concerns are addressed at the highest management levels.

The role of the workplace health and safety committees has been expanded. Committees continue to inspect their workplaces regularly and are also responsible for the investigation of complaints. Labour and management must make every effort to settle complaints themselves before a government Health and Safety Officer becomes involved.

Amendments to the right to refuse dangerous work streamlined the complaint resolution process by establishing an internal responsibility system that strengthens and clarifies the rights of both employers and employees. The employee will have the right to select a person from the workplace to participate in an investigation when a member of a health and safety committee is not available. Employees affected by a colleague's exercising his/her right to refuse dangerous work continue to receive their pay until the end of their shift or normal work period. The employer's investigation cannot be delayed should either party forego the right to be present. The employer has the right to discipline an employee found abusing the right to refuse dangerous work. However, the burden of proof rests with the employer. The employee may appeal to the Public Service Staff Relations Board.

Women who believe that their workplace presents a danger to their foetus or, in the case of nursing mothers, their baby, will have the right to remove themselves from the activity immediately and the employer must assign them to other duties until they obtain a doctor's certificate.

The employer has the right to assign the woman to other duties or require her to remain at work in a safe location.

These are some, but not all, of the changes to Part II of the *Canada Labour Code*. All are designed to strengthen labour-management self-governance over occupational health and safety and, in so doing, to make workplaces safer.

Supporting Material

Manager's Handbook Canada Labour Code Part II can be found on the TBS website under 'Occupational Safety and Health' at *www.tbs-sct.gc.ca/common/policies-politiques*

The Labour Program, Human Resources Development Canada website also provides information *http://labour.hrdc-drhc.gc.ca/*

Public Service Staff Relations Act (PSSRA) *http://laws.justice.gc.ca/en/P-35/*

2.13 Official Languages

English and French, Canada's two official languages, are distinguishing and important traits of Canadian society and of the Public Service of Canada. In many respects, linguistic duality is as closely linked to our collective identity as our democratic and legal institutions and our social programmes.

In keeping with the theme of the *Country Profile* series – management reform – the main and two-fold focus here will be on official languages in the federal public service, both from the point of view of service to Canadians and that of English and French as the official languages of work in the federal administration. The brief treatment here will go well beyond the limited scope provided in 1994, where the subject of official languages was only considered in terms of language training for staff.

The reader may find the initiatives described here of interest from either or both of the following perspectives: management reform within a particular federal programme, namely, official languages; and Canada's official languages programme. One can also view the discussion as a reflection of how the issue of official languages occupies a prominent place in the reform of public service management.

The Context for Change

There have been no legislative changes to the Canadian official languages model since the last edition of the *Canada Profile* in 1994 (the revised *Official Languages Act* was promulgated in 1988). However, fiscal belt-tightening in the early 1990s slowed down the implementation of the official languages programme, as happened with other federal programmes.

In recent years, the federal government has made a renewed commitment to official languages objectives. A key goal is to make the public service an exemplary workplace, whereby in certain designated regions, employees are fully able to work in the official language of their choice, as specified in the *Official Languages Act*.

Recently, there has been a conscious shift away from an over-reliance on a rules-based approach to one that puts a greater emphasis on the human dimension, on values such as respect and inclusiveness and on partnerships, notably by listening to and working with managers to address the challenges they meet in ensuring service in both official languages where required. This shift is contributing to a culture change within the federal government. In this approach, it recognises and counts on the abundance of goodwill among the various players.

The renewal includes work on identification of cultural and systemic barriers to the use of both official languages in the public service, a study of the perceptions and attitudes of public service employees toward official languages, and a streamlining and modernisation of policies, as well as efforts to increase the use of French in the workplace and the number of bilingual employees, and to balance representation of the two linguistic groups within the public service.

The projects, policies and initiatives discussed below seek to advance linguistic duality in Canada and the Public Service of Canada.

Best practices

Official Languages Action Plan

In spring 2001, the Prime Minister instituted a reference group of ministers, headed by the President of the Privy Council and Minister of Intergovernmental Affairs to prepare an action plan, which was tabled in early 2003. It lays out the programme's major streams for the years to come and states the means necessary to achieve the objectives. An exemplary public service, in terms of official languages, is one of its pillars.

Moreover, in 2001–2002 the Clerk of the Privy Council made the subject of official languages one of the five priorities deserving more sustained attention from deputy heads, a measure that will impact on all reporting levels.

Network of Official Languages Champions
A network of official languages champions, comprised of senior officials from federal organisations, act as agents of change, helping to advance official languages and making the renewal process more dynamic by bringing and stimulating leadership at the management level and ensuring the flourishing of official languages. During 2003, the champions will fine-tune their role and develop an action plan for their intervention strategy; this plan will include integrating official languages into all aspects of institutional operations, the development of generic tools and enhanced consultation on major issues.

Programme Monitoring
The Treasury Board Secretariat has a number of tools with which to monitor and report on programme implementation. For example, federal institutions submit to the TBS their annual official languages review, a public document approved by their most senior official. In consultation with members of the official languages network and the Office of the Commissioner of Official Languages, performance indicators will be developed which will further assist in the measurement of performance in various contexts such as the accountability accords for senior managers. Moreover, to evaluate their official languages performance, some institutions call upon the support of the local community. The TBS has conducted compliance audits and will continue to do so, as will the Commissioner of Official Languages. These and other tools will make it possible to monitor the programme more effectively and to identify issues for continuous improvement.

Perception and Attitude Study
In co-operation with other federal organisations, the Official Languages Branch of the TBS conducted a government-wide study on public service employees' attitudes and perceptions regarding official languages, particularly in the workplace. *Attitudes Towards the Use of Both Official Languages Within the Public Service of Canada* will assist in evaluating employees' levels of satisfaction, in identifying

barriers to the effective use of both official languages as prescribed by the *Official Languages Act* and to the improvement of attitudes, and in finding ways to raise the level of acceptance and use of both official languages in the workplace. Moreover, it will also be used to develop a new awareness strategy that aims to achieve long-term solutions culminating in a change of culture regarding a greater acceptance and use of both official languages in the Public Service of Canada.

Moreover, broader government-conducted employee opinion surveys in 1999 and 2002 (section 2.11) included an official languages component; the findings will help identify solutions to create a workplace more conducive to the enhanced use of both official languages, particularly of French, on a daily basis. These efforts will contribute to making the Public Service of Canada an employer of choice.

Language of Service

The *Official Languages Act* gives citizens the right to service in the official language of their choice. Official languages are thus taken into account in all service delivery channels of the federal government. More details are provided in the section of this volume on service. For example, Government On-Line is a major initiative designed to provide government services and information on the internet in both official languages. As a result of achievements to date, Canada is now a recognised world leader in this area. Via Service Canada access points (of which 17 have been designated as bilingual) and the 1-800 O-Canada telephone line, Canadians receive direct help and can quickly obtain information on more than 1000 federal programmes and services.

Language of Work

The Government of Canada is aiming to build an exemplary workplace with respect to official languages. That means a public service that not only provides high-quality services to Canadians in both official languages but also respects the linguistic rights of its employees. With the aim of promoting a workplace where respect for others forms the basis of interpersonal relations, particularly among Anglophones and Francophones, two pilot projects deserve mention, both within the Canada Customs and Revenue Agency, which has shown leadership in official languages matters.

The first pilot project, developed by the TBS, explored interpersonal respect and its application to English and French as languages of work. Two sets of workshops, involving 125 public service employees, led to fresh insights and a deepened commitment on the part of many to foster an increased use of French in communications between agency headquarters and offices in the province of Québec. Participants reported positive changes in themselves, in their work units and in inter-office communications from an official languages perspective.

The second pilot project at the agency focuses on processes: employees develop and implement mechanisms and tools necessary for a more equitable use of both official languages. This project is ongoing and the lessons learned from it will be applied elsewhere in the agency.

With regard to the use of English and French in the federal workplace, the Government of Canada counts on all concerned to promote a greater spirit of co-operation and openness, and encourages employees to consider it a civic duty to promote bilingualism.

Awareness Activities
The TBS has published an annotated version of the *Official Languages Act*, revised in partnership with the Department of Justice. Its explanations enable non-specialists to gain a better understanding of its application.

To better reflect the values and trends emerging from the activities and pilot projects of 2001–02, the course content of the official languages orientation, given country-wide, will be revised in 2003.

The TBS continues to provide information sessions to employees on service to public and language of work to better familiarise employees with the government's official languages objectives.

Best practices are increasingly being exchanged, with some posted on the TBS official languages website for broader dissemination.

To further integrate official languages into the day-to-day management of the institutions, the TBS continues to maintain and develop its networks of communication and exchange with departments and agencies, such as the network of official languages champions, the advisory committees of the departments and Crown corporations, the regional federal councils and the Interdepartmental Consultative Committee on Language Industries. Language industries include writing, translation, interpretation, language technologies such as speech processing, automated processing of written and spoken languages, electronic document management, technology and application software, and training and research, as well as jurilinguistics.

Supporting Material

Employee survey on official languages
www.tbs-sct.gc.ca/ollo/index_e.asp

The *Official Languages Act*
http://laws.justice.gc.ca/en/O-3.01/index.html

3 Service Improvement

3.1 Introduction

The Government of Canada's service agenda aims to improve the quality, effectiveness, timeliness and efficiency of Government of Canada services across all delivery channels (in person, on the telephone and on the internet) in both English and French – Canada's official languages. It also seeks to improve citizen and business access to these services. An important element of this agenda is the effective use of information and communications technology in enhancing services and service delivery.

Two operating principles guide service improvement in the Canadian federal government:

- Citizens and business must be at the centre of service delivery. To achieve this, improvements to services must be driven by the service needs and expectations of clients and focus on responding to the priorities for improvement that they have expressed through surveys, focus groups and other feedback mechanisms.

- A 'whole-of-government' approach is essential to drive citizen- or user-centred service delivery. The Government of Canada approach is centrally co-ordinated to achieve progress across the entire government; collaborative across departments and agencies, and across jurisdictions, involving the private and not-for-profit sectors; and transformative by encouraging the re-engineering, consolidation and integration of services where it makes sense.

While all departments and agencies are responsible for improving access to, as well as the quality and the range of services they provide, the TBS leads and co-ordinates the implementation of the government-wide service agenda.

The Context for Change

In 1998, the President of the Treasury Board reported to Parliament the government's new 'outside-in' citizen-centred approach to Government of Canada service delivery. This approach means basing service on citizens' needs and expectations instead of on what the organisation sees as important. Shortly thereafter, the Citizen-Centred Service Network, composed of 220 senior service delivery officials from the three orders of government in Canada, commissioned a public opinion research project (the Citizens First report) to document Canadians' expectations, satisfaction and priorities for service improvement.

The Service Improvement Initiative launched in 2000 addresses the challenge of improving citizen satisfaction with the quality of government service delivery. It set a minimum ten per cent improvement target for improved client satisfaction over the five years of the initiative for each key service to the public.

Government On-Line, an initiative announced in 1999 to deliver the Government of Canada's programmes, services and information over the internet, has become a key enabler for improving better access and service performance. The Government of Canada has set a target of putting the most frequently used services on-line by 2005.

In April 2002, the Government On-Line and Service Improvement Initiatives were integrated in recognition of the fact that an integrated, government-wide approach is needed to modernise and improve services for citizens and businesses no matter how, or in which official language, they choose to deal with the government. This integration supports the fundamental changes the government must make in the way in which it designs and delivers programmes and services if it is to remain relevant to Canadians.

Implementing Change

The Government of Canada is working in five key areas to support multi-channel service improvement and the delivery of on-line services. These areas are:

- Service transformation and multi-channel convergence – pursuing a user-centred approach to providing information and services to the people of Canada through the electronic, in-person and telephone service delivery channels;

- Common, secure infrastructure – building the electronic service platform to enable clustered services, interoperability and cross-channel convergence and to support secure electronic, telephone and in-person access;

- Policy and standards frameworks – addressing the issues of privacy, security and information management to build confidence in e-services and link service transformation to client satisfaction;

- Communications and marketing – encouraging take-up of electronic service options, reporting on progress and engaging citizens through various feedback mechanisms to shape the evolution of service delivery;

- Human resources – taking a cross-government approach to developing the right skills for the government's workforce to provide client-centred services across all service delivery channels.

In addition it has adopted a new policy on Alternative Service Delivery (ASD) to guide departments in assessing appropriate strategies and options for service delivery.

Supporting Material

Government On-Line and Canadians, 2002
http://www.gol-ged.gc.ca/rpt/gol-ged-rpt_e.asp

Sustainable, Secure Electronic Services – Building the Base for Government-Wide, Multi-Channel Service Transformation. Annual report on Canada's progress on GOL prepared for the 36th Conference of the International Council for Information Technology in Government Administration (ICA), 2002
http://www.gol-ged.gc.ca/pub/ica02/ica02-tb_e.asp

Departmental Performance Report for the period ending March 31, 2002. Treasury Board of Canada Secretariat, 2002
http://www.tbs-sct.gc.ca/rma/dpr/01-02/TBS/TBS0102dpr_e.asp

Citizens First. Citizen-Centred Service Network and the Canadian Centre for Management Development, 1998
http://iccs-isac.org/eng/cf-98.htm

Citizens First 2000. Public Sector Service Delivery Council and the Institute of Public Administration of Canada
http://iccs-isac.org/eng/cf-00.htm

*Results for Canadians: A Management Framework for the
Government of Canada.* Treasury Board of Canada Secretariat, 2000
http://www.tbs-sct.gc.ca/res_can/rc_e.html

*A Policy Framework for Service Improvement in the Government of
Canada.* Treasury Board of Canada Secretariat, 2000
http://www.tbs-sct.gc.ca/pubs_pol/sipubs/si_as/pfsi_e.html

A How-to-Guide for the Service Improvement Initiative. Treasury
Board of Canada Secretariat, 2000
http://www.cio-dpi.gc.ca/si-as/howto-comment/howto-comment_e.asp

3.2 Service Transformation and Multi-channel Integration

Service transformation and multi-channel integration involve pursuing
a user-centred approach to electronic, in-person and telephone service
delivery, driven by client priorities and expectations.

The Context for Change

Traditionally, information on government services has been organised
to reflect the structure of government. Accordingly, to access
information about a particular government service, Canadians were
required to know which department to contact in person, on the
telephone or through the internet. However, many Canadians are
uncertain about which department offers which service.

Implementing Change

In response to citizen demands, the Government of Canada has
completely redesigned its main internet portal, *www.canada.gc.ca.*
Launched in February 2001, the new website organises information
and services based on its three main client groups: individual
Canadians, businesses and international (non-Canadian) clients.

The Canadians Gateway provides information and services by topic
(for example learning about health care, filing income tax returns or
finding a job) and client group (for example youth or seniors). The
Business Gateway provides easy access to information and services that
a business might require over its life cycle from initial start-up to hiring
employees and exporting. The non-Canadians Gateway provides
information to foreign citizens who are interested in visiting, studying

or doing business with Canada, or who are interested in the country, its values and its involvement in international affairs. This client-centred approach removes the onus on clients to find and assemble related products from different government organisations, and provides access in one place to all information and services offered by the Government of Canada.

The Canada Site provides more than just information about government programmes and services. The site allows Canadians to interact with the government electronically, both to receive services and to express views. For example, Canadians can file personal income tax and benefit returns electronically, apply for employment insurance benefits on-line and notify the Canada Customs and Revenue Agency of a change of address through a protected website. Businesses can search for corporate names, register on-line for Canada Customs and Revenue Agency business programmes, incorporate federally and seek patent protection.

While the on-line 'service face' of the Government of Canada continues to evolve, progress behind the scenes is also evolving as a culture change of working horizontally is beginning to take hold. This involves moving from information and services that are grouped together to those that fit together and can be aligned in such a way as to facilitate simultaneous access.

Work has also advanced to provide a one-stop service using the in-person channel. The Service Canada Pilot Initiative, launched in 1999, put in place an integrated, government-wide approach to delivering Government of Canada services to Canadians. The pilot phase which included providing in-person single window access to basic information on Government of Canada programmes and services at select offices in communities across Canada was successfully completed in 2002 and responsibility for the maintenance and enhancement of the 122 Service Canada in-person centres was transferred to Human Resources Development Canada. In early 2003, there were 229 Service Canada in-person access centres across the country.

Finally, service standards are being established to ensure consistent and coherent service delivery across all channels.

Supporting Material

Government On-Line and Canadians, 2002
http://www.gol-ged.gc.ca/rpt/gol-ged-rpt_e.asp

Departmental Performance Report for the period ending March 31,
2002. Treasury Board of Canada Secretariat, 2002
http://www.tbs-sct.gc.ca/rma/dpr/01-02/TBS/TBS0102dpr_e.asp

Sustainable, Secure Electronic Services – Building the Base for
Government-Wide, Multi-Channel Service Transformation.
Annual report on Canada's progress on GOL prepared for the 36th
Conference of the International Council for Information Technology
in Government Administration (ICA), 2002
http://www.gol-ged.gc.ca/pub/ica02/ica02-tb_e.asp

3.3 Common, Secure Infrastructure

Establishing a common, secure infrastructure entails building an
enterprise-wide electronic service platform that enables integrated
services and supports secure internet, telephone and in-person access.

The Context for Change

Canadians expect affordable, accessible and responsive services. The
strategic use of information technology will enable the Government of
Canada to better meet these expectations.

Given the government's commitment to implementing a new electronic
face and to citizen-centred service delivery, it is critical that the
government's future investments in IM/IT (Information Management/
Information Technology) infrastructure is directed towards enabling this
vision. Of prime importance are those infrastructure components that
are needed on a government-wide basis. The development of common
and shared IM/IT infrastructure components for government-wide
application requires effective strategic planning and appropriate
governance.

Implementing Change

To achieve the required IM/IT infrastructure, the government adopted a
federated architecture approach for the strategic IM/IT infrastructure in
2000. Under this architecture approach, infrastructure elements are
planned, designed, co-ordinated and implemented into an integrated

and cohesive infrastructure of common government-wide IM/IT capabilities. This flexible approach also allows for groups of departments and department-specific infrastructures to interconnect with the common infrastructure as appropriate.

Planning for a common Government of Canada IM/IT infrastructure means defining how much common infrastructure is needed to meet both government-wide and departmental service delivery requirements. It also means defining the most effective and economical way to invest in, sustain and manage the necessary infrastructure.

Since 2000, the Government of Canada has been designing the guidelines and standards that will apply to the Government of Canada's IM/IT infrastructure to make systems interoperable across departments and agencies. Through its Federated Architecture Program, the government is pursuing an iterative, coherent, government-wide planned approach to the development of three main architectures:

- A technical architecture, to make IT systems and processes inter-operable while protecting privacy and strengthening the security of the Government of Canada's IT infrastructure;

- An information architecture, to facilitate the exchange of information between and among programmes to add value (for example convenience, faster turnarounds and greater accuracy) to transactions with external clients, and to ensure the government collects, stores, maintains and shares information in a coherent, standardised way to support more intelligent business operations;

- A business architecture, to enable programmes to be interoperable to support customised service delivery and to facilitate the reuse of processes and components to support more efficient operations and service delivery.

Taken together, these architectures constitute the Government of Canada's enterprise architecture. In concert with this design work, the initial phase of construction of the Government of Canada's Secure Channel is nearing completion. It is the key piece of common, secure infrastructure for all federal departments and agencies that will:

- Assure citizens that their information and transactions with government are protected;

- Assure citizens of the authenticity and integrity of government sites and databases;

- Protect against network intrusions;

- Provide on-demand, broadband network services to departments and agencies;

- Provide directory services;

- Provide identification and authentication of individuals and businesses with which government conducts business;

- Provide brokerage services and connectors to departmental enterprise-wide and administrative systems.

Together, these Secure Channel capabilities will enable clustered service delivery and the integration of voice and data, through a robust, scaleable IM/IT platform that supports multiple levels of security, including digital signatures.

During 2002–2003, key components of the Secure Channel, including an infrastructure for intrusion detection, directory services and the 'epass' service that enables on-line registration and authentication, have been implemented and are currently operating in Field Trial mode.

The 'epass' service, a key component of the Secure Channel, uses a combination of Secure Sockets Layer and Public Key Infrastructure technology to provide secure access to government programmes and is one of the world's first Public Key Infrastructure digital signature services for mass use by individuals. Each epass is unique and is used to authenticate the client and digitally sign documents. Epass is currently being piloted with Canada Customs and Revenue Agency's Address Change On-Line. As more on-line government services become available, it will be possible to use epass to access multiple programmes and services, including by businesses.

To facilitate interoperability and directly enable the provision of client-centred, integrated services, the Secure Channel includes a Service Broker, which acts as a service integration engine. It encompasses the 'middleware' between the distributed processes and systems of federal departments and agencies, and front-end client entry points such as the telephone, automated kiosks, in-person service counters and the government's internet portals and websites. The Service Broker acts as the 'technical translator', freeing up departments and agencies to focus solely on the business issues involved in horizontal service integration without having to worry about overcoming technological incompatibility issues and the costs associated with them. It also offers departments and agencies efficiencies, such as fully leveraging their investments in their current systems and delivering economies of scale from common application connectors.

By the end of 2003, it is expected that most federal departments will have migrated to the Secure Channel Network and be able to benefit from the enhanced functionality it provides.

Supporting Material

Chief Information Officer Branch (Treasury Board of Canada Secretariat) Website on Infrastructure
http://www.cio-dpi.gc.ca/inf-inf/index_e.asp

Sustainable, Secure Electronic Services – Building the Base for Government-Wide, Multi-Channel Service Transformation.
Annual report on Canada's progress on GOL prepared for the 36th Conference of the International Council for Information Technology in Government Administration (ICA), 2002
http://www.gol-ged.gc.ca/pub/ica02/ica02-tb_e.asp

3.4 Policy and Standards Frameworks

The provision of services on the internet necessitates the development and maintenance of appropriate policy and standards frameworks in the areas of privacy, security and information management to ensure seamless, clustered, secure and private service delivery. The revolution in information technology has also impacted on policies on access to information, communications, federal identity and official languages.

The Context for Change

Research shows that Canadians expect more from their government than they do from the private sector in terms of privacy and security, in large part because the government holds so much sensitive personal information about them, spanning their health, educational attainment, job history, utilisation of social benefits, and marital and financial status. Their perceptions about how seriously the government views its stewardship responsibilities for safeguarding their personal data and respecting their privacy will have a tremendous impact on the take-up of on-line services.

E-government and the concept of citizen-centred services have also created increased expectations in terms of the transparency of the affairs of those who govern in the public interest, and the speed and effectiveness of information transfer between the government and its citizens.

Information is an integral part of government service delivery and a cornerstone of government accountability. It must be managed as a strategic business resource from the earliest point in the business planning cycle through solution development, implementation, day-to-day business operations and assessments. All persons working for the Government of Canada use information in the conduct of their duties and have a responsibility and obligation for managing information. There is a need to improve the management of information in the Government of Canada to meet the additional challenges introduced by new service delivery paradigms and evolving technology, and to provide a focus for the implementation of information-related legislation and policies.

New service delivery paradigms and evolving technology have also resulted in a need to review and update existing policies on communications, federal identity and official languages.

Implementing Change

The Government of Canada is committed to protecting the privacy of Canadians and is recognised as a world leader in this area. To ensure that privacy protection is built right into the development or redesign of services, the Government of Canada became the first government in the world to adopt a Privacy Impact Assessment Policy. As of May 2002, Privacy Impact Assessments are mandatory for the design or redesign of programmes and services where there are potential privacy issues, such as those that may involve the increased collection, use or disclosure of personal information, the broadening of client populations, a shift from direct to indirect collection of personal information, and new data matching or increased reuse or sharing of personal information. The Privacy Impact Assessments promote fully informed policy, programme and system-design choices, and assist managers and decision-makers in avoiding or mitigating privacy risks. Recognising that transparency promotes confidence, summaries of the assessments are also required to be made publicly available. Moreover, as of 1 January 2004, Canada will have a comprehensive privacy regime that encompasses both the public and private sectors. This means that all transactions with citizens and clients/customers will be conducted in accordance with universal privacy principles. In this context, the Privacy Impact Assessments promote and render transparent good privacy practices.

On the security front, the Government of Canada has updated its Government Security Policy, which came into force in February 2002. The policy takes important new directions, calling on departments to meet baseline security requirements, to engage in continuous security risk management and to assure continuous service delivery. Departments and agencies are now being asked to think beyond traditional static defence strategies and approach information security as an ongoing and dynamic process. This means not only erecting layers of protective mechanisms but also being prepared to detect, respond to and recover from attacks that might take place against those protective mechanisms.

In August 2000, the federal government launched a comprehensive review of the access to information (ATI) framework with the objective of providing recommendations to modernise the ATI regime in ways that promote open, effective and accountable government, an informed citizenry and the public interest. The Task Force's report, released in June 2002, contains recommendations that take a uniquely integrated approach to ATI reform by addressing legislative, administrative and cultural issues.

The government is now working to modernise its existing information technology security standards regime, relying on information technology security expertise and best practices of its departments and lead agencies, as well as international standards bodies. Some 20 priority standards are in development.

Improving the state of information management, particularly the quality of information upon which service managers rely, is a key priority. The existing policy has been substantially revised to guide the efforts of departments and agencies to better align information management needs with modern business delivery requirements, including those associated with providing integrated, citizen-centred services. The Management of Government Information policy will help to accelerate the shift from a passive, records-based approach to a more dynamic, service-focused information management function that supports informed policy and decision-making and the delivery of high quality programmes, services and information through all channels.

To support the successful implementation of the policy, a Framework for the Management of Information in the Government of Canada has been completed and is now being further developed to provide practical guidance, and to set out the principles, standards and guidelines needed in an electronically enabled environment and to support electronic service delivery. For instance, the Dublin Core metadata standard and a core subject thesaurus have been adopted, and guidelines and controlled vocabularies are being developed for specific elements, including description, type, format, coverage and audience. The framework will include content management tools and further metadata standards for portals, gateways, clusters and websites to facilitate information access, retrieval and preservation, as well as reusing information across departments and agencies. The framework will also include guidelines for the long-term management of encrypted documents and digitally signed documents, as well as guidelines for the retention and disposal of electronic records. An Information Management Resource Centre website has been established for employees and business managers at all levels to provide a single point of access to Information Management instructional material, guidelines and standards, case studies and best practices.

Responding to the diverse needs of Canadians, the Government of Canada adopted a new communications policy in April 2002 designed to ensure that communications across the federal government are well co-ordinated and effectively managed. The Communications Policy of the Government of Canada takes account of an increasingly complex communications environment, addressing several important areas such as crisis and emergency communications, new technologies and official languages.

The government has also put in place additional requirements aimed at strengthening the presence and visibility of the Government of Canada in all its activities. These Federal Identity Program requirements address the issues of identifying the Government of Canada, applying the 'Canada' wordmark, identifying government facilities, identifying employees and communicating electronically.

One of these requirements includes the development of a common look and feel for all federal internet/intranet sites and electronic networks. These standards are designed to ensure that all Canadians, regardless of their internet ability, geographic location or demographic representation have equal access to information and services on

Government of Canada websites. The 33 standards approved in May 2000 fall into a total of seven categories and are intended to ensure outcomes such as federal websites that accommodate technologies such as text readers and voice-activated devices; a clear on-line federal identity so that Canadians know they are dealing with the Government of Canada; standardised and timely responses to citizen's e-mail enquiries; logical and consistent navigational formats; and compliance with all relevant policies of Canada's *Official Languages Act*.

In terms of official languages, a number of initiatives have been taken to advance linguistic duality in Canada and the Canadian public service. These include the preparation of an official languages action plan, the creation of a network of official languages champions comprised of senior officials from federal organisations to act as agents of change, the development of performance indicators to monitor the programme more effectively, and a study of perceptions and attitudes in the public service. With respect to technological developments and service delivery, the government's policy on alternative service delivery and its new communications policy both contain explicit official languages requirements.

Supporting Material

Privacy Impact Assessment Policy. Treasury Board of Canada Secretariat, 2002
http://www.tbs-sct.gc.ca/pubs_pol/ciopubs/pia-pefr/paip-pefr_e.html

Government Security Policy. Treasury Board of Canada Secretariat, 2002
http://www.tbs-sct.gc.ca/pubs_pol/gospubs/TBM_12A/gsp-psg_e.html

Access to Information: Making it Work for Canadians. Report of the Access to Information Review Task Force, 2002
http://www.atirtf-geai.gc.ca/report2002-e.html

Information Management Resource Centre Website
http://www.cio-dpi.gc.ca/im-gi/

Communications Policy of the Government of Canada. Treasury Board of Canada Secretariat, 2002
http://www.tbs-sct.gc.ca/pubs_pol/sipubs/comm/comm_e.asp

Federal Identity Program Policy, Treasury Board of Canada Secretariat, 1998
http://www.tbs-sct.gc.ca/pubs_pol/sipubs/tb_fip/arfip-espcim_e.asp

Common Look and Feel for the Internet Website
www.cio-dpi.gc.ca/clf-upe/

Official Languages Policies, Treasury Board of Canada Secretariat
http://www.tbs-sct.gc.ca/ollo/common/policies-politiques_e.asp

*Sustainable, Secure Electronic Services – Building the Base for
Government-Wide, Multi-Channel Service Transformation.*
Annual report on Canada's progress on GOL prepared for the 36th
Conference of the International Council for Information Technology
in Government Administration (ICA), 2002
http://www.gol-ged.gc.ca/pub/ica02/ica02-tb_e.asp

3.5 Communications and Marketing

Communications and Marketing are focused on encouraging take-up of
electronic service options, reporting on progress and engaging citizens
through consultations and other public opinion research mechanisms to
shape the evolution of service delivery.

The Context for Change

Communications with Canadians to ensure that their opinions and
needs guide the service agenda, to encourage use of on-line services
and to report on progress are critical to the success of the integrated
Government On-Line and Service Improvement Initiative.

Implementing Change

Public opinion research: The Government of Canada has engaged
and continues to engage a cross-section of Canadian society and clients
abroad in shaping this initiative. Public opinion research projects
covering a wide variety of topics, including how to better organise
information and services provided through the internet, service
priorities, security and privacy, and multi-channel service delivery,
are central to this approach.

Starting in December 2001, a representative panel of Canadian internet
users was assembled to provide important feedback and direction on
on-line service preferences and expectations. The first on-line survey
was completed with panel members in April 2002 and received 4547
responses. The survey themes included government service delivery;
personal information and the internet – privacy and security aspects;

web design and functionality issues; satisfaction with government websites; benefits of on-line services; and expectations of future on-line services. Five on-line focus groups were conducted in November 2002, allowing the government to examine some issues in greater depth including pre-testing new website designs, communications issues, and attitudes toward and expectations of on-line services.

Marketing: Promoting on-line services will be a priority in 2003–2004. These efforts will focus on using research to guide promotion and marketing initiatives to ensure that they respond to Canadians' service priorities and expectations while increasing take-up, and to promote increased awareness and understanding of the government's commitment to protect the privacy of citizens and ensure the security of their transactions.

To date, awareness of on-line services offered through the government's main internet portal, the Canada Site, has been attained through a variety of activities including fairs and exhibits, distribution of promotional materials, and television, radio, print and internet advertising.

Public reporting: Public reporting on Government On-Line plans and progress is critical to providing information to Canadians, as well as to keeping the private sector apprised of opportunities across departments. Each year the Government of Canada produces an overview report and each department publishes its plans and reports on its progress. These documents are available to the public on the Government On-Line website (*http://www.gol-ged.gc.ca/*) and on departmental websites.

GOL advisory panel: In September 2001, the President of the Treasury Board established an external advisory group made up of representatives from the private, academic and voluntary sectors to provide guidance in the implementation of the Government On-Line Initiative. This group, called the Government On-Line Advisory Panel, produced its second report on 11 December 2002. The report and its seven recommendations can be accessed at *http://www.gol-ged.gc.ca/pnl-grp/reports/second/transform/transform00_e.asp*.

Supporting Material

Departmental Performance Report for the period ending March 31, 2002. Treasury Board of Canada Secretariat, 2002
http://www.tbs-sct.gc.ca/rma/dpr/01-02/TBS/TBS0102dpr_e.asp

Sustainable, Secure Electronic Services – Building the Base for Government-Wide, Multi-Channel Service Transformation.
Annual report on Canada's progress on GOL prepared for the 36th Conference of the International Council for Information Technology in Government Administration (ICA), 2002
http://www.gol-ged.gc.ca/pub/ica02/ica02-tb_e.asp

Government On-Line Advisory Panel Website
http://www.gol-ged.gc.ca/pnl-grp/index_e.asp

3.6 Human Resources

Ensuring that employees have the knowledge, expertise, skills and competencies to deliver public services in an integrated, client-centred, multi-channel environment is a key factor in successfully delivering the Government of Canada's service agenda.

The Context for Change
Cultural change of the nature and magnitude required to deliver the government's ambitious service agenda must be led from within. Moreover it cannot be driven from the traditional human resources function alone. The development of horizontal relationships across the federal government, and support for community-led initiatives to address capacity issues and share work practices, is required.

Implementing Change
Strategies for change in human resources are being developed to support communities of practice in IT, IM and service delivery across federal departments and agencies. They focus on capacity-building, recruitment, retention and re-skilling.

The government supports the continued development of leadership and human resources in the IT community by developing the strategic components of a competency-based, community-led human resources framework for horizontal management of the government's IT human resources; assessing IM/IT management and executive development programmes; improving the generic staffing pools process of pre-qualified candidates for IM/IT executive positions; creating a repository of IT work descriptions for use in classification and staffing activities; and creating a web-based tool for information on project management training courses.

To provide a basis to build leadership and human resources of the IM community, the government has developed a vision that focuses on the special needs of this community and positions IM specialists as key enablers to policy development as well as service delivery. It has conducted an organisational modelling exercise to gather information on the state of IM at the departmental level and assess existing human resources capacity to meet the challenges that a fully enabled electronic environment presents for traditional work practices.

To encourage the development of key capacities in the service delivery community, a series of regional consultations have been held to identify the unique challenges of delivering integrated, citizen-centred services in the public sector and developing a sense of community. The government has also begun to design a service delivery practices database to share the critical knowledge needed to provide effective service delivery in an electronic environment.

Supporting Material

Organisational Readiness Office Website
http://www.cio-dpi.gc.ca/oro-bgc

Departmental Performance Report for the period ending March 31, 2002. Treasury Board of Canada Secretariat, 2002
http://www.tbs-sct.gc.ca/rma/dpr/01-02/TBS/TBS0102dpr_e.asp

Sustainable, Secure Electronic Services – Building the Base for Government-Wide, Multi-Channel Service Transformation. Annual report on Canada's progress on GOL prepared for the 36th Conference of the International Council for Information Technology in Government Administration (ICA), 2002
http://www.gol-ged.gc.ca/pub/ica02/ica02-tb_e.asp

3.7 Measuring Progress

Measuring progress on the integrated Government On-Line and Service Improvement Initiative is the key to moving forward and to demonstrating the ongoing value of investment. In 2002, the Government of Canada developed a performance measurement framework for these initiatives which encompasses three main outcomes: citizen/client-centred government, better and more responsive service, and capacity for on-line service delivery. For each of these outcomes, specific indicators have been developed, as follows:

Citizen/client-centred government	Better and more responsive service	Capacity for on-line delivery
• Convenience	• Critical mass of services	• Security
• Accessibility	• Take-up	• Privacy
• Credibility	• Service transformation	• Efficiency
	• Citizen/client satisfaction	• Innovation

Work is now underway to develop performance measures for these indicators, including a Common Measurements Tool (CMT) that will provide a consistent approach to be utilised across departments and agencies, for collecting client satisfaction information no matter which delivery channel is used. These tools will assist departments and agencies in meeting Government On-Line goals and delivering on the vision of improved, citizen-centred integrated services, including by facilitating efforts to identify priority areas for further investment. The first version of the CMT is available on-line through the Institute for Citizen-Centred Services, an intergovernmental research body dedicated to promoting excellence in public sector services and delivery channels (*http://www.iccs-isac.org/*).

Supporting Material

Sustainable, Secure Electronic Services – Building the Base for Government-Wide, Multi-Channel Service Transformation. Annual report on Canada's progress on GOL prepared for the 36th Conference of the International Council for Information Technology in Government Administration (ICA), 2002. *http://www.gol-ged.gc.ca/pub/ica02/ica02-tb_e.asp*

3.8 Organisational Forms and Alternative Service Delivery

Alternative Service Delivery refers to the many and varied organisational forms and delivery mechanisms that governments use to achieve their objectives. The Government of Canada has a long and successful tradition of deploying the full spectrum of ASD arrangements to deliver its programmes and services. The Canadian way is pragmatic and innovative but ultimately grounded in serving the public interest. A case-by-case approach helps to identify the delivery option that is most appropriate for the service and the setting. In this way, ASD helps to sustain a public service culture that reflects Canadian traditions of moderation, incrementalism, and diversity in institutional structures and incentives.

The Context for Change

ASD's modern roots can be traced to the Nielsen Task Force's recommendations on procurement and contracting out in the mid-1980s. The Bureau for Delivery of Programs and Services was established to pilot most efficient organisations and competition with the private sector. *Public Service 2000* changed the focus to improving the performance and reducing the cost of in-house delivery through semi-autonomous Special Operating Agencies (SOAs). Subsequent stocktaking resulted in SOAs being privatised, repatriated to departments or retained within tighter parameters. While SOAs plateaued federally at 20 agencies, many provinces and some cities adapted the concept successfully. The advent of ASD later produced higher-order service agencies for priority programmes.

In 1994–95, *Program Review* gave a new government a fresh start early in its mandate by systematically evaluating the design and delivery of all federal programmes. Under the banner, *Getting Government Right*, its legacy was an ongoing process of departmental self-examination of selected programmes and services. The Treasury Board issued a *Framework for Alternative Program Delivery* in 1995. ASD inherited much of the conceptual framework of *Program Review* but without the top-down target setting and the episodic adjustment in federal programming. There was no preconceived outcome, unlike the UK policy of creating a civil service of executive agencies or the New Zealand policy of wholesale commercialisation and privatisation of government entities.

ASD practitioners continued to be guided by the six test questions of *Program Review*:

1. Public interest – does the programme or area of activity serve the public interest?

2. Role of government – is there a legitimate and necessary role for the public sector in this area?

3. Federalism – is the current role of the federal government appropriate in this area?

4. Partnership – what activities or programmes should or could be provided, in whole or in part, by the private or voluntary sector?

5. Efficiency and effectiveness – if this programme or activity continues, how could it be improved?

6. Affordability – is the resulting package of activities or programmes affordable within the fiscal parameters of government?

Public service has changed dramatically since 1995. The Government of Canada has created more than 80 new ASD arrangements. Programme spending has decreased by $8 billion, from 16 to 12 per cent of GDP. At one time there were 55,000 fewer public servants. Only 45 per cent of federal public servants are engaged in direct service to citizens, instead of 75 per cent. It is estimated that 55 per cent of the public service operates outside traditional departments, making the 'alternative' now the norm.

The ASD portfolio in the Government of Canada includes a variety of delegated and collaborative arrangements:

• 18 SOAs (for example passports, consulting, training);

• Three legislated service agencies (food inspection, parks, revenue);

• 100 Crown corporations (for example financing, mail, broadcasting);

• 132 (2001 estimate) foundations and shared governance corporations (for example civil air navigation, airports, infrastructure);

• Numerous interdepartmental, intergovernmental and public-private partnerships (for example federal-provincial labour market agreements);

• Widespread outsourcing (for example military base support, real property management);

• Several employee takeovers (six in the national capital region);

• Selective privatisation (for example printing).

The most prominent ASD development since 1995 was the creation of three big service agencies: Canadian Food Inspection Agency (1997), Parks Canada (1998) and Canada Customs and Revenue Agency (1999). The Government of Canada rejected the notion of unbundling bureaucracy under a single agency model. All three agencies were established by enabling legislation, are responsible to ministers and report to Parliament as federal departments. Each operates under a different type and level of administrative authority, customised to its context and needs. While central agency policies do not always apply, these service agencies remain subject to their minister's policy direction and to Treasury Board approval of their business plan. They are separate employers, accounting for 35 per cent of employees in the public service.

Because they operate with greater autonomy and represent such a large portion of government, their actions set precedents, resulting in pressures and demands on core human resource, finance, and administrative regimes. They rely on innovative governance structures and management flexibilities to serve their mandates. At the same time, the agencies pose no challenge to ministerial and parliamentary accountability and still have considerable central agency oversight and guidance. The principles of modern comptrollership, applied through their planning and reporting processes, focus the agencies on citizen-centred service, public service values, results-based management and responsible spending. They help demonstrate how agency form can be used to find the right balance between autonomy and accountability in institutional arrangements.

Implementing Change

Central responsibility for ASD is housed in the Treasury Board of Canada Secretariat. The Treasury Board approved a new *Policy on Alternative Service Delivery* effective from 1 April 2002. Its purpose is to guide departments in assessing appropriate strategies and options for service delivery. The policy recognises that ASD arrangements must conform to the public interest and contribute to good governance. Government's renewed commitment to ASD encourages innovation, strengthens Treasury Board oversight of new initiatives, improves reporting to Parliament on new governance arrangements and ensures that the public service as an institution learns from experience. Consistent with *Results for Canadians*, ASD practice is becoming more results focused, citizen-centred, transparent, accountable and values driven.

The Government of Canada is rethinking the form and function of its new policy in favour of a less regulatory and more collaborative approach to policy administration. To fulfill its central role, the Treasury Board Secretariat is building a 'community of practice', is establishing itself as a 'centre of expertise' and is evolving as a 'virtual organisation'. It has developed policy, guidance and a comprehensive website to support the federal framework and to complement departmental capabilities. This initiative stems in part from observations by the Office of the Auditor General that the Treasury Board needs to extend its management board role and professional capacity to support emerging ASD arrangements. It responds, in particular, to the proliferation of new delegated forms (for example foundations) and collaborative practices (for example horizontal management) across government.

There is an unprecedented opportunity to apply ASD expertise to governance and service delivery challenges in Canada and abroad. ASD is distinctly Canadian, reflecting the texture and size of the country and its place in the world. Its diversity of perspectives is a strength in creatively generating ASD innovations, in producing a track record of results and in influencing international applications. At the same time, practitioners continue to grapple with the implications of globalisation, information technology, public service renewal and citizen-centred service delivery. They are challenged in scoping ASD, in sharing best practices, in accessing support groups and in capitalising on networking synergies. There is an immediate need to build capacity to respond to demands emerging for national and international co-operation. ASD remains integral to 'getting service delivery right'.

Supporting Material

Ford, Robin and Zussman, David (eds.) (1997). *Alternative Service Delivery: Sharing Governance in Canada*. Toronto: Institute of Public Administration of Canada and KPMG Centre for Government Foundation.

KPMG and Public Policy Forum (eds) (2000). *Change, Governance and Public Management: Alternative Service Delivery and Information Technology*. Ottawa: Public Policy Forum.

Treasury Board of Canada Secretariat Alternative Service Delivery (sub-site). Ottawa: Treasury Board Secretariat
http://www.tbs-sct.gc.ca/asd-dmps

Wilkins, John K. (2000). 'Alternative Service Delivery Mechanisms', in Public Sector Group (eds), Administrative and Civil Service Reform (website). Washington, DC: The World Bank.
http://www1.worldbank.org/publicsector/civilservice/alternative.htm

Zussman, David (2002). 'Alternative Service Delivery', Chapter 4 in Christopher Dunn (ed.), *The Handbook of Canadian Public Administration*, pp. 53–76. Don Mills: Oxford University Press.

4 Stewardship

4.1 Introduction

Under the guiding principles of *Results for Canadians*, the aim of stewardship is good value for public expenditure and better results for Canadians. This is achieved through federal resources that are appropriately aligned with government priorities, and used efficiently and effectively with prudence and probity and through clearly defined and public reporting of key commitments and results. Government departments and agencies continually strive to achieve these outcomes through strengthened management practices and accountability, better allocation of resources, and results-based performance that demonstrates responsible spending and adherence to public values and ethics.

The Context for Change

Canada's vision of modern public management has evolved over several decades and will continue to do so. Over time the focus of effort has shifted, but the changes form a continuum. Each effort has built on the strengths and accomplishments of the initiative that went before. In the late 1970s and the mid-1980s, after a period of unprecedented policy development and departmental growth, the focus was on improved management practices and controls. In the mid-1990s, the main focus was on improving Parliamentary reporting and increasing the transparency of public spending. By the late 1990s, the need to improve services to citizens became a priority. As the decade drew to a close, the need to fundamentally rethink human resources management became the focus.

Implementing Change

The table on page 81 provides a sense of the key events and improvements that have taken place within the federal government of Canada since

1994 in an effort to strengthen stewardship across the public service and to increase excellence in management practices.

Modern comptrollership delivers on a key benefit: the increased effectiveness of the government in fulfilling its mission and achieving objectives. It represents better management.

Independent Review Panel Report

In this period it was realised that the divide between programme management and specialised functions like finance and information technology was no longer absolute, and that all managers needed to apply sound management practices that were previously the domain of specialists. This was the origin of the Modern Comptrollership Initiative, conceived in 1997 by an independent panel convened to review the future of comptrollership. The panel concluded that comptrollership could no longer remain a specialist function. The panel described modern comptrollership as a 'set of principles founded on a philosophy'. The philosophy is that stewardship must become part of every manager's thinking and behaviour, and that to exercise responsible stewardship a manager's decisions should bring together integrated financial and non-financial performance information, sound risk management, options for flexible delivery with due regard for appropriate control, and sound public service values and ethics.

The goal of the federal government is to improve management practices in all these areas and to achieve excellence in management through a modern management agenda.

While the objectives of stewardship remain constant, the means of achieving them are guided by revised government priorities, new insights as a result of continuous learning, and new opportunities and ways of doing business. To this end the Government of Canada has embarked on a series of modernisation initiatives in pursuit of achieving tangible *Results for Canadians* in the domain of management excellence. This includes:

a) Improving performance through modern comptrollership and integrated risk management, including rigorous stewardship, appropriate controls, and shared values and ethics;

b) Improving the allocation and re-allocation of financial and other resources to better align resources to the highest priorities, as well as the management of resources in the delivery of programmes;

Chronology of Stewardship Initiatives, 1994–2003

1994   The federal government initiated an extensive programme review to confirm the relevance and affordability of programmes, and the appropriateness of programme delivery mechanisms.

The federal government introduced a new expenditure management system to provide better control of overall spending levels, more focus on long-term departmental plans and better information for Parliament.

1995   The federal government initiated a project to implement its Financial Information Strategy (FIS) and announced in the Budget Plan of the Minister of Finance the government's intention to adopt full accrual accounting, a key component of FIS.

1996   The federal government introduced a new planning, reporting and accountability structure (PRAS) to provide departments and agencies with a basis to plan, manage and communicate performance information to parliamentarians.

1997   The federal government announced a reorientation of the Treasury Board to a Management Board with a mandate to refocus attention from specific transactions to wider issues of direction and business plans.

A federally commissioned Independent Review Panel on Modernization of Comptrollership in the Government of Canada tabled its final report, which was accepted by the Management Board.

1998   A Comptrollership Modernization Pilot project was launched, with the voluntary participation of 15 departments.

2000   The federal government:
- developed and adopted a new management framework – *Results for Canadians*;
- developed and promulgated a policy for grants and contributions which requires a results-based accountability framework that includes performance indicators, expected results and outcomes, and evaluation criteria to be used in assessing the effectiveness of the programme;
- developed and promulgated a policy on Contaminated Sites and Solid Waste Landfills Inventory.

2001   The federal government:
- approved the government-wide implementation of modern comptrollership;
- developed and adopted a new Risk Management Framework;
- developed and promulgated a revised policy on internal audit;
- developed and promulgated a revised policy on evaluation.

2002   The federal government:
- developed and promulgated new policies on federal contaminated sites management and the accounting for costs and liabilities associated with federal contaminated sites;
- developed and promulgated a revised policy on alternative service delivery.

2003   The federal government announced in its February Budget that it is moving to full accrual accounting and that the 2002–2003 financial statements will be audited on that basis.

c) Improving ongoing information management for better decision-making through more relevant and timely evaluations and internal audits;

d) Strengthening public accountability and reporting of results-based management, with integrated financial and non-financial information, using accrual accounting as the basis for financial management and reporting;

e) Improving the management and stewardship of assets, such as real property.

Some Lessons Learned

Most of these modern management initiatives have some common key elements for success. These include the following:

• All the initiatives require central leadership to provide the overall direction and co-ordination needed to make improvements in 90 organisations, individually and collectively, to make government-wide progress. This overall leadership includes the formulation of enabling policies and the creation of governance structures that leverage collective wisdom and knowledge and obtain necessary commitments to move in agreed upon directions and timeframes.

• Almost all the initiatives required incremental funding to ensure that they were properly launched and nurtured. Approximately $200 million of one-time incremental funding was provided in total for FIS and modern comptrollership implementation, strengthening the evaluation and internal audit functions, and enabling the implementation of the new policy on the management of contaminated sites. This was in addition to internal reallocation of existing resources – many times more than the amount of incremental funding – within each of the organisations for these and the other initiatives to improve modern management. Some the funding was used to provide centres of excellence, address common areas of need such as building capacity, undertaking common research, and building and sharing common tools and guides. A specific Modern Comptrollership Innovation Fund was established to promote joint undertakings to this end.

• In terms of building capacity, significant efforts and products were devoted to communications and continuous learning – recognised as critical success factors in change management. Each of the web pages referenced in this section provides extensive coverage of these areas and of the many other factors that cannot be presented in this document.

In the end, the commitment and efforts of many individuals, on their own and with others in their own and other organisations, are the most essential elements contributing to success in all the initiatives identified above. Departments and agencies have steadfastly devoted people and resources to achieving all these objectives, while meeting their programme responsibilities. Their individual websites provide additional information on these many modern management change initiatives.

While significant benefits continue to accrue from current efforts to improve management practices, more has to be done. As a result, while the Government of Canada continues to implement all these initiatives for change, it will be initiating additional measures to further improve government-wide stewardship over the coming years. The following pages provide highlights of many of these initiatives.

Supporting Material

Website for the Treasury Board Secretariat
http://www.tbs-sct.gc.ca/index_e.asp

Website for the Comptrollership Branch of the Secretariat
http://www.tbs-sct.gc.ca/organisation/com-con_e.asp

Gateway to the sites of government departments and agencies
http://canada.gc.ca/depts/major/depind_e.html#A

4.2 Managing Expenditures

Managing expenditures concerns the allocation of financial and other resources by central agencies to departments, and in turn to specific programmes and activities, as well as departments' own management of resources in the delivery of their programmes. The Government of Canada manages expenditures in part through the Expenditure Management System (EMS), which was introduced in February 1995. This section describes the evolution and operation of the EMS up to 2002, placing particular emphasis on the role played by the Treasury Board of Canada and its Secretariat.

The Context for Change

The federal government began a string of annual deficits in fiscal year 1970–71, contributing to a steady rise in the debt-to-GDP ratio from its post-war low of 18 per cent in 1974–75. By the end of 1992–93, the deficit had grown to over $41 billion (5.9 per cent of GDP), and the debt-to-GDP ratio stood at 67 per cent. By this point, there was growing awareness in the federal public service, on international financial markets and among the Canadian public that the government needed to take swift and significant action – particularly by reducing expenditures – in order to avoid the kind of fiscal crisis that New Zealand had faced in the 1980s.

The Liberal Party, who were to win the general election of 1993 and form a majority government, also recognised the need for reductions and promised, as part of their election platform, to reduce the deficit-to-GDP ratio to 3 per cent by 1996–97. This promise was followed in early 1994 by an announcement in their first budget that this objective would be achieved in part by reducing expenditures following a process of reviewing the spending of all departments.

This announcement led, among other things, to the Program Review exercise of 1994. Under Program Review, the government examined $52 billion in direct programme spending (accounting for 32 per cent of overall spending) to assess the relative priority and cost-effectiveness of programmes, and ultimately to identify candidates for reduction and restructuring. A central feature of this examination involved asking six questions about every programme:

1. Is it still in the public interest?

2. Is its delivery a legitimate and necessary role for government?

3. Is the current federal role appropriate, or should the programme be realigned with the provinces?

4. Should it be delivered in partnership with the private or voluntary sector?

5. Can it be redesigned for efficiency?

6. Is it affordable, given fiscal constraints?

The results of the review, announced in the 1995 budget, were substantial: a total of $16.9 billion in savings over three years, reducing planned programme spending by almost 19 per cent by 1997–98. A second Program Review exercise was conducted in 1995, which led to the announcement of an additional $1.9 billion in savings over three years in the 1996 budget. These two sets of budget decisions put the government on track to achieve its deficit-to-GDP target of 3 per cent by 1996–97, and even to achieve a further reduced target ratio of 2 per cent by 1997–98.

As Program Review cuts were considered permanent (and not to be reversed in the future), both reviews also anticipated significant ongoing savings after their three-year implementation periods. Nevertheless, having put programme spending on a permanent downward track through reductions in direct programme spending and other expenditures, the government then needed a budget process which ensured that this track was not subsequently tilted upwards by the addition of altogether new direct programme spending measures. To accomplish this, in early 1995 the government formally adopted a renewed budget process called the Expenditure Management System (EMS). Two key features of the new EMS were the elimination of central policy reserves and the requirement that departments finance new initiatives by re-allocating funds from existing programmes. Ongoing review of programmes by departments was to ensure that funds went towards the highest priorities and most cost-effective programmes, without increasing net spending levels.

While ministers of line departments retained authority over and responsibility for spending in their portfolios, they were required to inform Treasury Board ministers of the details of (and proposed changes to) departmental spending through a 'Business Plan'. Following the final budget decisions by the Prime Minister and the Minister of Finance, and the tabling of the budget in February, departments would prepare Business Plans that provided detail on how they would implement those budget decisions (including requested re-allocations and managerial authorities). Business Plans replaced a number of old internal reporting documents and outlined, for the upcoming three fiscal years and within approved expenditure levels:

• Major challenges, directions and objectives within the context of government priorities and departments' current and prospective positions;

• Strategies, actions, associated costs and the flexibilities required to deal with major changes;

- Associated goals, targets, and performance measures to assess programme results and management strategies.

At the same time, the Minister of Finance adopted a much more prudent approach to his management of the government's 'fiscal framework' (aggregate revenues and expenditures). This new approach had two main elements. The first was to make greater use of private sector forecasts of economic activity, and to deliberately favour conservative interpretations of those forecasts when estimating certain future revenues and expenditures for planning purposes. The second element was to set aside $2–3 billion every year in a contingency reserve, to be spent only if revenues still fell short of expectations or in case of a very large and unforeseen expense, failing which the entire amount would lapse (and so reduce the actual deficit for that fiscal year). The Minister of Finance's conservative estimates of governmental revenues helped dampen departmental expectations of new funding and provided effective top-down discipline of overall government spending, and his contingency reserve lapsed in full every year, which further aided deficit (and later debt) reduction.

Departments produced business plans on an annual basis from 1995 to 1998. During this period, two observations were made. The first was that the performance information contained within the plans was of variable quality. Departments often submitted variations on their Reports on Plans and Priorities (RPPs) which, as documents aimed at a general and public audience, contained information that was less precise, less disaggregated and less closely linked to actual departmental operations than the TBS desired. The second observation was that the TBS lacked the capacity to fully review and analyse each of the more than 70 plans it received from departments. As it became evident that business planning was not significantly helping the TBS to better manage the government's resources, the requirement that all departments submit an annual business plan to the Treasury Board was phased out from 1999.

By this time, the deficit had been reduced to zero and new funds were again available for spending on programmes (as well as for reducing taxes and retiring debt). Some of these funds were allocated to new initiatives that responded to policy pressures that had accumulated since 1995. Another portion was allocated to address operational pressures in existing programmes that had accumulated over the same period. Through an exercise known as Program Integrity, which was conducted in 1999 and again in 2000, the TBS identified many critical risks to the continued achievement of results in the delivery of existing programmes and services across government, assessed whether strategies were in place to mitigate those risks, and explored various funding options. The Treasury Board was then able, through the policy and budget priority-setting processes, to secure funding that could in turn be allocated to departments, over multiple years, to address critical pressures and to facilitate the restructuring of departmental programmes and budgets.

Nevertheless, due to new policy commitments and pessimistic economic forecasts, there was not enough flexibility in the fiscal framework to fully address all of the pressures that the TBS identified. So the Prime Minister asked ministers to find ways of adjusting their programmes and budgets so that departmental operations would be sustainable within existing funding levels.

In April 2001, the government introduced the concept of a 'Departmental Assessment' (DA) submission that would provide departments with an opportunity to outline how they planned to accomplish this (for example by scaling back or eliminating existing programmes or by delivering existing programmes more efficiently), as well as to outline the possible consequences in terms of service delivery – particularly over the long term – and the possible policy and political implications. The TBS was to work with departments during the preparation of their DAs in order to ensure that restructuring and reallocation options were sustainable, and that the risks and consequences had been properly identified. For its part, the Treasury Board was to consider granting the authority necessary to implement departmental adjustment strategies, and refer to Cabinet or the Prime Minister those proposals that had significant policy or political implications. Participation by departments in the DA process was, however, voluntary and by the end of 2002 very few departments had identified themselves as candidates and prepared or submitted a DA.

Implementing Change
In preparation for a fiscal year that begins on 1 April, the government typically tables a budget in Parliament in February. There are four major components of the government's 'budget': the Minister of Finance's budget speech (which outlines the government's overall fiscal policy, as well as major changes to revenue and expenditure measures); the Main Estimates (containing more detailed information on the

requested appropriations for each department); the Reports on Plans and Priorities (through which departments provide performance information on the expected costs, activities and results of their programmes); and the actual legislation (primarily the Appropriation Bills) on which Parliament votes.

A simplified version of the current EMS, paying particular attention to the role of the TBS, would identify three major inputs to budget decisions on expenditures. The first input concerns the renewal (for one more year) of existing spending on programmes and the addition of recently-approved funding. Beginning in July, the TBS calculates, for each department, the size of their budgets for the upcoming fiscal year (and, for planning purposes, for the two subsequent years). This calculation takes into account ongoing spending from previous years, sunsetting funds and new funding approved by the Treasury Board since the previous budget exercise (see 'Treasury Board submissions' below). Departments indicate how new funding will be apportioned to their various programmes and how ongoing funding may be reallocated among programmes. This exercise is known as the Annual Reference Level Update (ARLU), which culminates in the production of the Main Estimates and the Appropriation Bill. No process is in place by which ongoing expenditures across government are comprehensively or systematically reviewed or challenged by the central budget agencies for continued relevance or cost-effectiveness, although individual departments may conduct their own reviews, either as part of, or separate from, the budget process.

The second input concerns the addition of new funding, most often for new programmes designed to implement initiatives outlined in a Speech from the Throne. Throughout the year, departments will use Memoranda to Cabinet (MCs) to propose new policies (see section 5). Most such MCs receive approval in principle from one of the two Cabinet policy committees – the Cabinet Committee on the Social Union (CCSU) and the Cabinet Committee on the Economic Union (CCEU). In December and January, the Prime Minister and the Minister of Finance determine which of these initiatives will receive funding in the budget, and to what extent. These two decision-makers may also include in the budget funding for initiatives that had not been previously submitted to one of the policy committees for approval in principle. (In most cases, departments must subsequently submit an MC that receives approval in principle before they may access those funds.)

The new funds are then announced in the budget speech, but often are not included in the Main Estimates or other budget documents since final decisions may be made too late for this.

The third input concerns statutory expenditures. Projected statutory expenditures for the upcoming year are included in the budget not for approval, but simply for information, because statutory expenditures have, by definition, already been authorised, often for an indeterminate period of time, by Parliament in the original legislation. Nevertheless, statutory expenditures, for example payments on the debt, benefits for the elderly and transfer payments to the provinces, are important as they make up roughly two-thirds of annual expenditures. Again, there is no process in place by which statutory expenditures are comprehensively or systematically reviewed or challenged by the central budget agencies for continued relevance or cost-effectiveness, but the Department of Finance and individual departments may conduct their own reviews. As votes in Parliament on budget legislation are deemed matters of confidence in the government – and as a 'no' vote could force new elections – Parliament typically adopts the government's budget legislation without changes.

Important budgetary decisions are also made during the fiscal year covered by the budget. Such decisions may be made through at least three related processes.

1. *Treasury Board submissions.* When new initiatives are announced in the budget, the Department of Finance notionally sets aside the associated funds in the fiscal framework for the appropriate departments. However, departments may not actually spend these funds until the Treasury Board has approved detailed plans that outline how the initiatives will be implemented through specific programmes. Departments may prepare such submissions at any time in the fiscal year. The TBS analyses these submissions and makes recommendations to the Treasury Board. The TBS may recommend that special conditions be placed on the funds, such as requirements that they be spent only for very particular purposes or that they may not be released until the department has provided the TBS with certain information. In rare instances, the TBS may recommend that the Treasury Board should not approve the submission.

2. *Supplementary Estimates.* Two or more times a year, the TBS prepares additional appropriations legislation relating to the current

fiscal year. New initiatives that are announced in the budget are not always sufficiently detailed, in terms of how the funds will be allocated to specific departments, to be included in the initial Appropriations Bill and voted on by Parliament. In these cases, funds are notionally set aside in the fiscal framework but are not added to the 'reference levels' of specific departments. Thus, once departments have received Treasury Board authority to spend these funds (through a Treasury Board submission), they must return to Parliament during the fiscal year to receive legislative authority to spend. The Supplementary Estimates process provides an opportunity for the government to detail and obtain parliamentary approval of the precise allocation of new funding announced in the budget to specific departments and, occasionally, to detail and obtain Parliamentary approval for new funding not announced in the budget. If time is of the essence, departments may be allowed to access (and spend from) a special Treasury Board-managed fund until the legislation is passed, at which point they reimburse the fund. Supplementary Estimates are also used to update Parliament on the government's actual expenditures on statutory programmes.

3. *Reserve management.* The Treasury Board manages two reserves which departments may petition to access in order to address operational pressures on their programmes. For example, an aspect of a department's operations may pose a significant risk to the health or safety of its employees or the public, or may require bridging finance in anticipation of a more permanent policy or funding decision. Another Treasury Board-controlled reserve is aimed at addressing pressures related to increases in departments' expenditures on salaries due to the outcomes of collective bargaining. Additionally, the Department of Finance controls a reserve aimed at addressing pressures related to unanticipated and non-discretionary increases in expenditures in certain quasi-statutory programmes, and the Privy Council Office controls a reserve aimed at addressing pressures related to threats to public security and anti-terrorism efforts. (Accessing these reserves requires, in addition to approval by the relevant central agency/agencies, a request in the Supplementary Estimates since, with the exception of the Compensation Reserve, all these funds are simply notionally set aside in the fiscal framework, and are not appropriated to the government by Parliament through the Main Estimates.)

After 27 years of consecutive annual budgetary deficits, the federal government has posted surpluses in each of the last five fiscal years. Forecasts of future revenues and expenditures suggest that this string of surpluses will continue at least into the near future. Nevertheless, economic forecasting is still a very inexact science and unforeseen events that require an immediate – and often expensive – response from the government are not uncommon. Fiscal discipline is still required to ensure that the government does not return to a deficit situation. At the same time, however, the government must respond to changing priorities and emerging knowledge, which often requires an increase in spending on certain activities. To help the government achieve the twin objectives of fiscal discipline and policy responsiveness, in early 2003 the TBS began to develop plans to play a more effective role as part, along with the Department of Finance and the Privy Council Office, of the Government of Canada's 'budget office' network.

There are four key components of the TBS's potential budget office role (in the annual budget cycle). The first involves gaining detailed and government-wide knowledge of the expected costs and results of departments' programmes. The TBS can gain this knowledge by improving the reporting relationship and pattern of dialogue between the TBS and all departments across government. The second involves gaining in-depth and up-to-date knowledge of specific expenditure and management issues in departments. The TBS can gain this knowledge through targeted and selective reviews of specific organisations, programmes and horizontal policy areas in government. The third component involves informing Treasury Board ministers of expenditure and management issues in the government. The TBS can accomplish this by analysing the information gained from reporting, dialogue and reviews; by synthesising key risks and opportunities from a government-wide perspective; and by presenting findings and recommendations to Treasury Board ministers. In particular, the TBS may focus on ways of better aligning resources with government priorities and expected results through the reallocation of resources (both within and between departments), and through the transformation of programme structures. The fourth component involves consolidating reserves under the Treasury Board and developing a single set of allocation criteria, and giving the Treasury Board more authority as to how new funds announced in the budget are allocated to specific departments and programmes.

Finally, a parallel initiative concerns the use of accrual information and techniques in federal budget-making. As part of its commitment to better financial management, the government is currently implementing accrual accounting through the Financial Information Strategy (see section 4.7). The government is also reviewing the potential of accrual budgeting to determine if it would provide a better framework for resource management. The findings of this review will be incorporated into the government's ongoing review of the EMS.

Supporting Material

Aucoin, Peter and Donald J. Savoie, eds. *Managing Strategic Change: Learning from Program Review.* Ottawa: Canadian Centre for Management Development, 1998 (available for order at the following website:
http://www.ccmd-ccg.gc.ca/research/publications/index_e.html)

Canadian government websites
  TBS: *www.tbs-sct.gc.ca*
  Finance: *www.fin.gc.ca*
  PCO: *www.pco-bcp.gc.ca*
  Parliament: *www.parl.gc.ca*
  Auditor General: *www.oag-bvg.gc.ca*
  Bank of Canada: *www.bank-banque-canada.ca*
  Main portal: *www.canada.gc.ca*

4.3 Modern Comptrollership

As a management reform, modern comptrollership is one of the government's key priorities and is focused on the sound management of public resources and effective decision-making.

Modern comptrollership goes to the heart of the Government of Canada's management framework as described in *Results for Canadians*. Simply put, in its quest to achieve the highest quality of service to the public, the Government of Canada is committed to excellence in four areas that are critical to a well-performing public sector: citizen focus, values, results and responsible spending. Canadians expect continuous improvement in management practices and increased focus on results, responsible spending and accountability.

While traditional comptrollership focuses primarily on financial information, modern comptrollership supports the effective stewardship of resources of all types throughout the federal government with greater attention to results for Canadians. It is about working smarter for better results: *better informed decisions, better public policies and better service delivery*. Modern comptrollership is intended to provide managers with integrated financial and non-financial performance information, a sound approach to risk management, appropriate control systems and a shared set of values and ethics.

There are two specific dimensions to modern comptrollership – people and infrastructure. On the people side, roles and responsibilities related to comptrollership have evolved for managers and functional specialists. The people challenges are:

- To build awareness and acceptance of these changing roles and responsibilities;
- To articulate the requisite modern comptrollership competencies and skills;
- To self-assess the extent to which the competency profile is met;
- To develop learning plans to build the required capacity.

In terms of infrastructure, organisations must create an environment conducive to modern comptrollership and provide the appropriate delegations of authority, mature integrated information systems, appropriate controls, and tools to support their managers and functional specialists to manage in this complex reality. Modern comptrollership is also about a different relationship between departments and agencies and the Treasury Board Secretariat as the Government of Canada's management board.

The Context for Change

In 1997, the Independent Panel on Modernization of Comptrollership in the Government of Canada, which the federal government had earlier commissioned, issued its report, which was fully adopted by the government as a blueprint for modernisation, resulting in a three-year modern comptrollership pilot project, followed by a decision in 2001 for government-wide implementation by 2005.

This panel defined modern comptrollership as a set of principles founded on a philosophy. The philosophy is straightforward. The stewardship of public resources can no longer remain the domain of functional specialists; it must become a management function.

Managers should be able to discharge their stewardship responsibilities without resort to overweening 'command and control' policies. And in consequence of this, a new partnership should exist between functional specialists and programme managers based on a mutual commitment to integrated management decision-making.

From this philosophy, the panel derived four principles, sometimes referred to as the four pillars of modern comptrollership. The choice of the term 'pillar' could be misleading since it connotes rigidity and separateness when in fact the four should be seen as dynamic systems and modes of management practice. In a fully effective organisation, each would function in its own right, and all would enjoy a dynamic interrelationship one to another.

The panel proposed that the four principles should be viewed as the essential prerequisites of integrated decision-making. Every modern manager, from the front line to the executive committee table, must be capable of making decisions that bring together integrated financial and non-financial performance information, sound risk management, options for flexible delivery with due regard for appropriate control, and sound Public Service values and ethics.

Integrated Financial and Non-Financial Performance Information: Measuring and reporting on performance is not a simple matter for governments. All over the world, different jurisdictions are struggling to improve the quality of the performance information provided to citizens. Modern comptrollership assumes this commitment to performance reporting, and then goes one better. Modern comptrollership assumes that departments can not only report on their programme performance but can also, in a relatively systematic fashion, link the resources spent with the results achieved. It is understandable that parliamentarians will want to know what it costs to produce certain results. But managers also need to know what it may cost to produce a result. Why? Because there are alternative ways of doing so, each with differing costs, and being able to associate resources with results makes for more informed choices about the most cost-effective course.

Sound Risk Management: Risk, together with cost, needs to be prominent in the analysis of options since the level of risk one is prepared to manage has a bearing on the real cost of achieving the result. Every manager to some degree relies on instinct to factor risk into the choices he or she makes. But this is not sufficient. Every well-performing organisation owes it to its managers to systematically consider the risk environment within which it must operate, the tolerance that the organisation has to risk, and the guidance and latitude it is prepared to give its managers.

Appropriate Control: Faced with diminishing resources and mounting demands for public engagement and accountability, modern managers must continually seek out innovative ways to deliver results for Canadians. But being able to do so presumes that managers are provided with an integrated, principles-based framework of appropriate internal control in place of a multiplicity of overly complex control policies. Again, the issue of risk management must be considered in establishing what is 'appropriate' control because the extent to which control can be released is dependent on the extent to which there is tolerance of risk. If there is zero tolerance of risk, there will be a rigid and comprehensive control framework.

Values and Ethics: Finally, every decision by managers in the Public Service of Canada must be grounded in the values of the public service and of their department. This is not a hypothetical matter. The ethical standards of public service in Canada are among the highest in the world. Every day, however, public servants are challenged to make complex choices. From their departments, they require guidance and tools on applying public service values in making complex, day-to-day decisions.

None of the four 'pillars' is new, and singly each does not make comptrollership 'modern'. It is recognition of their interdependency and management of their interrelationship that transforms and 'modernises' comptrollership.

Responsibility and Entitlement: Managers should approach the pillars in two ways: as a personal responsibility and as a professional entitlement. First, it is the responsibility of every manager to ensure that his or her management practices manifest the four principles. Every manager should strive to make decisions that bring together risk management, appropriate control, resources and results, and public service values and ethics. At the same time, however, managers should feel entitled to expect from their department an integrated framework and agenda for risk management, systems that link financial and non-financial performance information in a timely and accessible manner, integrated control frameworks and practical guidance on the application of ethics and values in day-to-day decisions. In turn it is the obligation of modern, effective organisations to provide to their managers an environment conducive to the practice of modern comptrollership principles.

Implementing Change

During 1998–2001 13 departments and two agencies took part in the pilot phase of modern comptrollership. As organisations embark on implementing modern comptrollership, an assessment tool known as the 'capacity check' is available to departments and agencies to perform a self-assessment of current capabilities relative to modern comptrollership management practices. This baseline assessment, involving interviews with executives and managers, allows for the identification of priority areas for improvement (i.e. processes, competencies, systems, etc.). Results from departmental assessments, combined with other management reports and performance information, are used to identify departmental priorities for

---

The criteria used for the capacity assessment are:

Core Criteria

Shared Values and Ethics
- Values and ethics framework

Mature Risk Management
- Integrated risk management
- Integrated management control framework

Integrated Performance Information
- Integrated departmental performance reporting
- Operating information
- Measuring client satisfaction
- Service standards
- Evaluation information
- Financial information
- Cost management information

Rigorous Stewardship
- Business process improvement
- Management tools and technique
- Knowledge management
- Accounting practices
- Management of assets
- Internal audit
- External audit

'Enabling' Criteria

Strategic Leadership
- Leadership commitment
- Managerial commitment
- Senior departmental functional authorities
- Planning
- Resource management
- Management of partnerships
- Client relationship management

Motivated People
- Competencies in modern management practices
- Employee satisfaction
- Enabling work environment
- Sustainable workforce
- Valuing peoples' contributions

Clear Accountability
- Clarity of responsibilities and organisation
- Performance agreements and evaluation
- Specialist support
- External reporting

---

improvements and develop action plans to address them. These priorities will depend on particular departmental circumstances, respective businesses, client needs and other considerations.

The pilots demonstrated that the successful implementation of modern comptrollership depends on managers' ability to:

- Provide strong leadership;
- Motivate employees;
- Strengthen control systems and monitoring;
- Share best practices;
- Focus on results.

With the decision in 2001 to implement modern comptrollership government-wide, every department and agency is now expected to integrate modern comptrollership as a key element of their management improvement agenda, but each has flexibility on the timing and approach. An organisation is ready to start modernising when:

- The Deputy Head and senior management are committed and engaged;
- A plan is in place to integrate modern comptrollership with ongoing management improvement initiatives;
- There is awareness and understanding of modern comptrollership within the organisation;
- The organisation, given its other priorities, has the capacity and ability to implement modern comptrollership.

The process begins with designation of a project leader by the Deputy Head and the development of a broad strategy for integrating modern comptrollership into the organisation's management improvement agenda. In most cases, a dedicated project management office is also required. The size of the project management office will depend on the size of the organisation and the effort required to build the momentum and integrate comptrollership modernisation. At a minimum, a designated project leader is required, even if no formal office is established. This individual or group will work with senior management and other groups in the organisation to co-ordinate modernisation efforts.

Once an approach and strategy have been decided, the next step is to assess the current state of modern comptrollership in the organisation.

For this purpose, a comptrollership capacity assessment tool has been developed and tested during the pilot phase. It allows an organisation to perform a self-assessment of modern comptrollership capacity. The assessment process is flexible but typically it covers everything relating to modern comptrollership throughout the organisation, including horizontal issues. The capacity assessment will provide the basis for creating a comptrollership modernisation action plan, or adding features to the organisation's overall management improvement framework and action plan.

To stimulate government-wide adoption of modern comptrollership, a Comptrollership Innovations Fund has been established with an annual budget of $10 million for fiscal years 2001–02, 2002–03 and 2003–04. These resources are intended to help offset the initial costs of modernising comptrollership. Funding is available for project management offices, comptrollership capacity assessments and selected key projects.

Approximately 90 organisations are involved in comptrollership modernisation under the leadership of the Treasury Board and its Secretariat.

Supporting Material

Report of the Independent Panel on Modernisation of Comptrollership in the Government of Canada
http://www.tbs-sct.gc.ca/cmo_mfc/resources2/review_panel/rirp_e.asp

Modern Comptrollership
Central web page
http://www.tbs-sct.gc.ca/CMO_MFC/index_e.asp
Start up tools and information
http://www.tbs-sct.gc.ca/cmo_mfc/resources_e.asp
   A Guide to Getting Started
   Suggested Steps for Modernising Comptrollership
   Communicating Modern Comptrollership
   Capacity Assessment
   Action Plan Guide
   Governance Structure

Changing Management Culture: Highlights of a Symposium on Modern Comptrollership and Cultural Change
*http://www.tbs-sct.gc.ca/CMO_MFC/Communications/Symposium_*
report/sr_e.asp)

4.4 Risk Management

The Context for Change

The Integrated Risk Management Framework delivers on the commitment set out in *Results for Canadians – A Management Framework for the Government of Canada* (March 2000) to strengthen risk management practices within the public service. In doing so, the Integrated Risk Management Framework supports the four management commitments outlined in *Results for Canadians*: citizen focus, values, results and responsible spending. The Integrated Risk Management Framework advances a citizen focus by strengthening decision-making in the public interest and placing more emphasis on consultation and communication. Similarly, it respects core public service values such as honesty, integrity and probity at all levels, and contributes to improved results by managing risk proactively. Integrated risk management also supports a whole-of-government view grounded in rational priority setting and principles of responsible spending.

Implementing Change

Responding to the need to strengthen risk management as a priority on the government management agenda, the TBS led research and consultations on risk management in collaboration with federal organisations, academics and private interests. The results highlighted the need for a common understanding of risk management and a more corporate, systematic approach. Informed by knowledge and experience from the public and private sectors in Canada and internationally, the Secretariat and its partners collaborated on the development of an Integrated Risk Management Framework.

The framework is designed to advance the development and implementation of modern management practices and to support innovation throughout the federal public service. It provides a comprehensive approach to better integrate risk management into strategic decision-making. It provides organisations with a mechanism to develop an overall approach to manage strategic risks by creating the means to discuss, compare and evaluate substantially different risks on the same page. It applies to an entire organisation and covers all the risks it faces (in the fields of policy, operations, human resources, finance, law, health and safety, and environment).

The purpose of the Integrated Risk Management Framework is to:

• Provide guidance to advance the use of a more corporate and systematic approach to risk management;

• Contribute to building a risk-smart workforce and environment that allows for innovation and responsible risk-taking while ensuring that legitimate precautions are taken to protect the public interest, maintain public trust and ensure due diligence;

• Propose a set of risk management practices that departments can adopt, or adapt, to their specific circumstances and mandate.

Application of the framework is designed to strengthen management practices, decision-making and priority setting to better respond to citizens' needs. Moreover, practising integrated risk management is expected to support the desired cultural shift to a risk-smart workforce and environment. More specifically, it is anticipated that implementation of the framework will:

• Support the government's governance responsibilities by ensuring that significant risk areas associated with policies, plans, programmes and operations are identified and assessed, and that appropriate measures are in place to address unfavourable impacts and ensure that the organisation benefits from opportunities;

• Improve results through more informed decision-making by ensuring that values, competencies, tools and a supportive environment form the foundation for innovation and responsible risk-taking, and by encouraging learning from experience while respecting parliamentary controls;

• Strengthen accountability by demonstrating that levels of risk associated with policies, plans, programmes and operations are explicitly understood, and that investment in risk-management measures and stakeholder interests are optimally balanced;

• Enhance stewardship by strengthening public service capacity to safeguard people, government property and interests.

Integrated risk management respects and builds on core public service values. Outcomes of applied integrated risk management must be ethical, honest and fair; they must respect laws, government authorities and departmental policies, and result in the prudent use of resources.

The Integrated Risk Management Framework responds to the recommendations contained in the *Report of the Independent Review Panel on Modernisation of Comptrollership in the Government of Canada* (1997) and its call for a strong commitment to four key elements: performance reporting (financial and non-financial); sound risk management; the application of an appropriate system of control and reporting; and values and ethics. In identifying as a priority the strengthening of risk management across the Public Service, the report stressed the need for:

> ... *executives and employees* [to be] *risk attuned – not only identifying but also managing risks ... matching more creative and client-driven decision making and business approaches with solid risk management ...*

and

> ... *creating an environment in which taking risks and the consequences of doing so are handled within a mature framework of delegation, rewards and sanctions.*

The framework builds on existing risk-management practices, reflects current thinking, best practices and the value of well-recognised principles of risk management. It is linked with other federal risk management initiatives across government, including recent efforts to strengthen internal audit and evaluation and increase focus on monitoring. Risk-management frameworks are also being developed in areas such as legal risk management and the precautionary approach. Collectively, these individual initiatives are contributing to strengthening risk management across the federal government in line with modern comptrollership and to improving practices in managing risk from a whole-of-government perspective. These initiatives will also contribute to improving the way government manages its programmes and services and meets the needs of Canadians.

The framework is a practical guide to assist public service employees to think more strategically and improve their ability to set common priorities.

The framework is comprised of four elements:

- Developing the corporate risk profile;
- Establishing a risk management function;
- Practising integrated risk management;

• Ensuring continuous risk-management learning.

Departments and agencies are actively working to implement the framework. The framework is being implemented in phases, then rolled out to all departments and agencies over time, based on lessons learned from pilot implementation. The Treasury Board Secretariat Centre of Expertise for Risk Management is providing overall guidance and advice to help departments and agencies implement the framework as well as identify and share risk management best practices.

Supporting Material

Risk Management Central Web Page
http://www.tbs-sct.gc.ca/rm-gr/home-accueil.asp?Language=EN

Integrated Risk Management Framework
http://www.tbs-sct.gc.ca/pubs_pol/dcgpubs/RiskManagement/rmf-cgr_e.asp

Best Practices in Risk Management
http://www.tbs-sct.gc.ca/rm-gr/category-categorie.asp?Language=EN &site=RMD&id=010

4.5 Strengthening Evaluation and Internal Audit

The Context for Change
As a follow-up to the 1997 R*eport of the Independent Panel on Modernisation of Comptrollership in the Government of Canada*, the TBS initiated separate, but parallel, reviews of the two existing policies for internal audit and evaluation. The reviews included consultations throughout the process with deputy ministers, heads of internal audit and evaluation, and other senior public service and private sector managers. The reviews identified the need for better-positioned internal audit and evaluation functions government-wide, which would also contribute significantly to the achievement of the government's management agenda tabled in Parliament in March 2000, *Results for Canadians: A Management Framework for the Government of Canada*. The result of both reviews is improved policies on internal audit and evaluation. In 2001 the government announced its revised policies.

Implementing Change

Evaluation

The revised evaluation policy gives evaluation a central role, distinct from that of internal audit. It also places a greater emphasis on evaluation as a management function that provides objective information on the results of programmes and initiatives that affect Canadians. At the same time, a Centre of Excellence for Internal Audit and a Centre of Excellence for Evaluation have been established within the TBS in order to provide leadership, advice and support to departments for the successful implementation of these policies.

The revised policy on evaluation and its standards emphasises the role of evaluation in providing timely, objective information on the performance of government policies, programmes and initiatives. It is intended to help managers achieve better results for Canadians by stressing the need for sound evaluation. The main highlights of the revised Evaluation Policy are that it:

- Establishes a stand-alone policy and evaluation function (it is now separate from the Internal Audit Policy and its function);

- Expands the policy to evaluate the success of programmes, policies and initiatives in meeting their objectives (the previous policy refers primarily to the evaluation of programmes);

- Broadens the scope to include departmental, interdepartmental and intergovernmental considerations (the previous policy stresses departmental programmes);

- Stresses the need for managers to embed the discipline of evaluation in all their work, including the design of new policies, programmes or initiatives.

During the intervening period leadership and support has been focused on assisting organisations reposition evaluation as a key management tool; several millions of dollars have been allocated to do this. Evaluation networks have been created or re-established to provide ongoing government-wide sharing of information and experiences and extensive guidance has been offered to assist managers and evaluators on the development of evaluation frameworks as an integral part of ongoing management practices. To support capacity building, a community development strategy has been designed, competency profiles and an internship programme have been developed, and a training and development curriculum for evaluators has been established. Capabilities to monitor the health of evaluation government-wide, and track trends and issues across the system have also been established. Much work still remains to be done and many challenges will have to be tackled over the next few years. Plans are being developed to successfully address these.

Internal Audit

The revised internal audit policy repositions the internal audit community within government as a provider of independent assessments to departmental senior management on all important aspects of risk-management strategies, management control frameworks and information used for decision-making and reporting.

The revised policy on internal audit and its standards are aimed at providing independent assessments (or 'assurance') of the soundness of risk-management strategies, management control frameworks and information used for decision-making and reporting. Other highlights of the revised internal audit policy are summarised below:

- It requires an active audit committee chaired by a senior departmental executive;

- It ensures that departmental heads of internal audit have an unimpaired ability to carry out their responsibilities, including reporting audit findings;

- It requires that internal auditors have unlimited access to all departmental documents;

- It requires that management action plans adequately address the recommendations contained in internal audit reports and that they are implemented.

During the intervening period leadership and support has been focused on assisting organisations to strengthen internal audit as a key management tool; a considerable amount of funding has been allocated to do this. A small agency initiative to assess the risks and issues has been established and a four-year government-wide strategic plan has been developed in consultation with the internal audit community. In support of capacity building through the renewal of a skilled workforce and the provision of guidance, competency profiles and human resources and learning strategies have been developed. A nationwide competition was held to identify qualified candidates for staffing. More opportunities for consultation and information sharing have been put in place (for example semi-annual Heads of Internal Audit Retreats) and more structured forums, such as quarterly Internal Audit Network meetings and monthly Senior Advisory Committee meetings are taking place to provide ongoing government-wide sharing of information and experiences. Internal audit guides and other internal audit tools have also been developed and distributed. Much work remains to be done and many challenges will need to be tackled over the next few years. Plans are being developed to successfully address these.

These combined policies on evaluation and internal audit therefore require that:

- Departments develop annual internal audit plans and evaluation plans, and make all completed internal audit and evaluation reports easily accessible to the public in both official languages;

- Departmental managers incorporate the findings of internal audits and evaluations into their priority setting and decision-making;

- The Treasury Board makes a significant investment to support these initiatives to assist organisations appreciably increase their capacity to improve performance in each of these key functions.

Supporting Material

Evaluation central web page
http://www.tbs-sct.gc.ca/eval/home_accueil_e.asp

Evaluation Audit Policy
http://www.tbs-sct.gc.ca/pubs_pol/dcgpubs/TBM_161/ep-pe_e.asp

Internal Audit central web page
http://www.tbs-sct.gc.ca/ia-vi/home-accueil_e.asp

Internal Audit Policy
http://www.tbs-sct.gc.ca/pubs_pol/dcgpubs/ia-vi/pia-pvi_e.asp

4.6 Performance Reporting

The Context for Change
Performance reporting is a key integrating principle of *Results for Canadians* and a variety of initiatives have been underway, in

conjunction with all the other efforts to enable organisations to focus on the achievement of results and to report them in simple and understandable ways to elected officials and to Canadians. Efforts have been concentrated in two primary areas: reporting on individual programmes and on horizontal initiatives.

Implementing Change

Departmental Planning, Priorities and Performance Reporting

Each year approximately 86 Departmental Performance Reports (DPRs) for the Government of Canada are tabled in Parliament. They outline the achievements of individual departments and agencies measured against the commitments in their respective Reports on Plans and Priorities (RPPs). These play a key role in the cycle of planning, monitoring, evaluating and reporting results through ministers to Parliament and Canadians. They provide parliamentarians and Canadians with a comprehensive accounting of results.

Organisations have been asked to produce an effective public planning report that meets the following criteria:

- It serves as an important planning instrument that has clear, concise and credible information that aids parliamentarians in meeting their decision-making responsibilities;

- It serves as an instrument of public accountability that demonstrates to Canadians what they receive in return for their tax dollars, in accordance with the funding that Parliament authorises for each federal department and agency;

- It serves as an instrument of public engagement, providing the foundation for a dialogue between citizens and their government on its future plans and directions;

- It provides evidence of sound management and demonstrates that public reporting on plans is consistent with internal planning processes and strategic and operational plans.

Organisations have also been asked to produce performance reports that respect the following reporting principles:

- Provision of a coherent and balanced picture of performance that is brief and to the point;

- Their focus should be on outcomes, not outputs;

- Performance should be associated with earlier commitments, and any changes should be explained;

- Performance should be set in context;

- Resources should be linked to outcomes;

- It should be explained why the public can have confidence in the methodology and data used to substantiate performance;

- They should include a report on horizontal indicatives, for example modern comptrollership and sustainable development.

Continuous efforts to assess and improve the quality of information provided in these reports are being made and over time the government is confident that through continuous learning and improvements in such areas as modern comptrollership, risk management, evaluation and internal audit, the reporting of programme information will improve.

The government is continually improving its tools and looking for ways to accelerate the pace of improved accountability and reporting. For example, the TBS has established a Strategic Outcomes Database that can be used to link such outcomes by programme and organisation. Information such as this is expected to provide organisations with better understanding of linkages that will lead to better performance reporting and better decision-making.

Performance Reporting on Horizontal Issues

For the first time in December 2001, a report was published on Canada's performance. This is a very comprehensive report that includes information on as many as 19 societal indicators that reflect a balance among social, economic and environmental themes. The indicators are grouped into four main themes: economic opportunities and innovation, health, environment, and the strength and safety of communities. This report is a reference tool that is intended to help Canadians to better evaluate the Government of Canada's performance and to play a greater role in developing public policy. The Government of Canada believes that a strong democracy like Canada's is built on the active engagement of its citizens and their understanding of the country's social and economic issues.

An updated edition of the report, *Canada's Performance 2002* highlights Canada's strengths as well as the areas in which it can do better. The information in this report shows there have been successes in the health field. Improvements are especially evident in terms of life expectancy and infant mortality rates. In the last decade, life expectancy at birth has steadily increased from 77.3 years in 1989 to nearly 79 years in 1999. Infant mortality has fallen from 7.1 to 5.3 deaths per 1,000 live births in the same period. Canada's economy has also demonstrated solid performance, especially in employment. However, the results also indicate that some segments of the population are still living below the poverty line and that Canada faces challenges with respect to the environment and the need for a more involved civil society. *Canada's Performance 2002* is a unique report as it establishes links between federal programme performance and socio-economic outcomes, while also allowing a comparison to be made between Canada and other countries.

The themes and societal indicators are:

1. *Economic opportunities and innovation:* real gross domestic product per capita, real disposable income per capita, innovation, employment, literacy and educational attainment.

2. *Health:* life expectancy, self-rated health status, infant mortality and physical activity.

3. *Environment:* air quality, water quality, biodiversity and toxic substances in the environment.

4. *Strength and safety of communities:* volunteering, attitudes toward diversity, cultural participation, political participation and safety and security.

Improvements in the 2002 report include the addition of a 'Performance Highlights' section, summarising Canada's performance over several years in each of the areas covered. The report also includes more disaggregated data than the first edition. For example, there are breakdowns by region, by gender and by groups of Canadians such as Aboriginal peoples and new immigrants. To facilitate government-wide analysis, the report also groups departments and agencies that work towards similar objectives within each theme. Through links to a database, the electronic version of the report provides access to departmental reports on plans and priorities, departmental performance reports, and audit and evaluation information.

The report is an important tool for demonstrating the government's commitment to overall performance, accountability, transparency and the effective use of public funds.

Supporting Material

Canada's Performance 2002

http://www.tbs-sct.gc.ca/report/govrev/02/cp-rc_e.html

Horizontal Results

http://www.tbs-sct.gc.ca/rma/eppi-ibdrp/hr-rh_e.asp

Results-based Management

http://www.tbs-sct.gc.ca/rma/rbm-gar_e.asp)

Departmental Estimates, Reports on Plans and Priorities and Performance Reports

http://www.tbs-sct.gc.ca/est-pre/estime.asp

4.7 Accrual Accounting/ Financial Information Strategy

The Context for Change

While accounting standards continue to evolve to present economic reality more accurately, there is nevertheless a broad continuum ranging from cash to full accrual accounting. In the early 1990s the federal government had begun work on a Financial Information Strategy which envisioned moving from a modified cash/accrual system of accounting to a system of full accruals where tax receivables are recorded and capital assets and inventories are charged as an expense when used, thereby providing for a more complete recognition of liabilities.

The Independent Review Panel on Modernization of Comptrollership in the Government of Canada, the Public Sector Accounting Board of the Canadian Institute of Chartered Accountants, the Auditor General of Canada, the International Federation of Accountants and others have advised the Canadian government to adopt full accrual accounting because it provides a more complete measure of the overall size of the government, allows financial results to be presented on a more appropriate and widely recognised accounting basis, allows the financial results of the government to more adequately reflect the economic realities of the period in question and, with proper and better information on assets and liabilities, enables managers to make better decisions and do a better job of managing resources.

Implementing Change

Accrual Accounting

The Minister of Finance first announced the government's intention to adopt full accrual accounting in the 1995 Budget as part of the federal government's Program Review and in November 1995, the Treasury Board ministers approved the FIS as a government-wide project to implement the strategy. Since then, central agencies and government departments have been working to lay the necessary infrastructure of policies, systems and expertise to implement this reform.

By April 2001 all departments and agencies had successfully implemented full accrual accounting as part of the FIS and since then every department and agency has been preparing their own financial statements on an accrual basis. For various reasons, however, the government decided, at the time, not to produce its Public Accounts and Financial Statements on a full accrual basis.

With the 2003 February Budget, the federal government announced that it will implement its commitment to present its consolidated financial statements on a full accrual accounting basis, thereby providing a more comprehensive accounting of its assets and liabilities, presenting a more transparent picture of the government's financial position and enhancing accountability, the management of liabilities and the stewardship of assets.

The major effects of the adoption of accrual are:

- All tax revenues will be reported in the year they are earned rather than when the amount is received. They will be recorded as receivables or as refunds payable, rather than recorded when the cash transaction takes place.

- Liabilities that were not previously reported will be recorded when they are determined to be likely and estimable, rather than when the cost occurs. They are now recorded as liabilities later in time.

- Capital assets and inventories will be recorded as assets when purchased and the amortisation or utilisation will be recorded as an expense. In the past, non-financial assets were not reported, so that acquiring real property or inventory would show as expenditures, but the asset would not show in the balance sheet.

- Implementing accrual accounting will result in a retroactive restatement of the financial statements previously reported. Various asset and liability balances and the accumulated deficit will be restated to reflect the new accounting policies. Therefore this change will also affect the calculation of the financial indicators of the government's financial position and results such as the annual surplus and the accumulated deficit.

Full accrual accounting is part of the government's Financial Information Strategy. The adoption in the government's financial statements is the last milestone in this initiative.

Financial Information Strategy (FIS)

FIS represents a government-wide initiative to enhance decision-making and accountability across government, and to improve organisational performance through the strategic use of financial and non-financial performance information. It is a prerequisite of the introduction of accrual accounting and to the success of both modern comptrollership and *Results for Canadians* as it directly supports three of the four key elements of modern comptrollership, and the information it provides is fundamental to linking expenditures with results. However, FIS is not so much about accounting as about accountable decision-making and its ultimate success will occur when programme managers and other non-financial specialists become adept at using and applying good financial and non-financial performance information in their daily decision-making to improve accountability and organisational performance. Focusing on people, policies and systems are all necessary for success. While all of these present significant challenges, the key is not number crunching, but managing for results.

People

A governance structure was established to provide the direction and oversight to implement all the necessary changes centrally and in over 90 organisations within the established parameters and timeframe. This included distinct accountabilities for the successful implementation within individual organisations and central administration. The deputy heads were accountable for implementation within their own organisations and the TBS and Public Works and Government Services Canada had accountabilities for government-wide implementation. The TBS had overall management responsibilities, including policies, and PWGSC was responsible for the central accounting systems. A government-wide FIS senior management steering committee was established to provide overall direction and co-ordination and an FIS Forum was established to set up individual working groups to deal with specific details and technical matters of common interest and concern. Special efforts were also put in place to manage the significant cultural change accompanying this significant undertaking.

A comprehensive learning strategy and framework was produced, as well as training packages for delivery at the work place and at training institutions. In addition a government-wide communications strategy, plan and framework were also produced for both government-wide use and for use by specific organisations. The internet was used extensively for collecting and disseminating information and many presentations and forums were used to collect and share ideas and information. In addition, a framework and plan were developed to directly address the change management elements of FIS. These included wide-range discussions, plans and documents to identify and provide concrete material on what to expect and how to ease the transition to the new FIS environment.

Policies and Systems

Until FIS, the financial statements of government organisations were prepared centrally using central accounting systems operated by PWGSC. With FIS, accountability for financial statements was transferred to individual organisations with the central systems used only to capture and report summary data. Hence, in addition to the change to accrual accounting, there were many other significant changes to manage. This not only required close collaboration between policy makers and systems designers but also extensive training of practitioners and managers. Areas most affected by FIS and accrual accounting included capital assets, inventories, prepaid expenses, tax receivables, environmental liabilities, and retirement and employee benefits.

With respect to systems, each federal organisation was required to have in place by 1 April 2001 a financial and administrative system capable of producing its financial statements on a full accrual accounting basis in the manner prescribed by the TBS. In addition, the central accounting systems, operated by PWGSC, were also required to be in full compliance with accrual accounting requirements, and to be able to collect summary information from the departmental systems and produce the annual Public Accounts and Financial Statements for the

Government of Canada. Working together, all departments and agencies were able to install new financial systems that could handle the accrual accounting requirements of FIS and create the interfaces needed to transmit summary financial information to the central systems. All these systems were successfully made FIS-compliant by the established target date of 1 April 2001.

During the 1990s there were over 40 financial and administrative systems in government departments and agencies and efforts were made to gain efficiencies and improve effectiveness by reducing this number. At the time of adopting FIS, the number of approved systems had been reduced to seven and all organisations were required to use one of these approved systems to meet their FIS obligations. As a result cluster groups were established to collectively manage the federal government's involvement with these systems. While the system was still complicated, the reduction in the number of systems dramatically increased the probability that each organisation could have a fully compliant FIS system by the established target date. However, this required continual and close collaboration to identify, resolve and test all the technical challenges. In spite of all the obstacles, over 90 organisations were able to meet their FIS obligations, while at the same time tackling the challenges of mitigating risks associated with the Y2K 'millennium bug'.

To properly move to accrual accounting the federal government amended its accounting standards and revised or issued a number of policies, including allowances for valuation of assets and liabilities, contingent liabilities of the Government of Canada, accounting for fixed assets and inventory, accounting for inventories and receivables management. It also issued a *Financial Information Strategy Accounting Manual* and provided guidelines and associated training so that all departments and agencies would be able to prepare their own financial statements using full accrual accounting.

Since the completion of FIS on 1 April 2001, accrual accounting poicies have been issued and followed, new financial information systems have been installed and are now operational, accounting expertise needed to report on the greater range of financial activity has been acquired and all assets have been valued so that an opening balance for inventories could be included in the 2002/2003 period 01 financial statements.

As indicated earlier, following on from the final steps to introduce accrual accounting, the federal government has established a working group on accrual budgeting to examine the potential application of accrual information to the budgetary process. The working group is examining how accrual concepts bear on many types of decisions, drawing on the experience of other governments that have implemented accrual accounting. For the present, appropriations by Parliament remain unchanged.

Supporting Material

Financial Information Strategy Web Page
http://www.tbs-sct.gc.ca/fin/sigs/FIS-SIF/FIS-SIF_e.asp)

List of associated standards and policies
http://authoring.tbs-sct.gc.ca/fin/common/al_ina_e.asp

Impact of accrual accounting on the Federal Government's financial statements
http://www.fin.gc.ca/budget03/bp/bpa6e.htm

4.8 Improving Real Property Management

The Context for Change

In 1995, when the federal government decided to adopt accrual accounting, it also established the position of Commissioner of the Environment and Sustainable Development as an integral part of the Office of the Auditor General of Canada to encourage stronger performance by the federal government in the areas of environment and sustainable development. The Commission's mandate is to make the government accountable for greening its policies, operations and programmes, and to assist parliamentarians in overseeing the federal government's efforts to protect the environment and foster sustainable development. Canada is one of the very few countries in the world with an Environment Commissioner reporting to the legislature and the only one whose Commissioner has a formal audit mandate.

Accrual accounting requires that all assets be identified and valued, and sustainable development requires that all assets be identified and managed in a manner consistent with sustainable development policies and directions. Hence, these two 1995 decisions, together with the overall objectives of *Results for Canadians*, have been key drivers in the way in which federal government departments manage their real property assets.

Implementing Change

These two drivers of change have significantly altered how real properties are valued and managed across the public service.

Until the completion of FIS in 2001, the federal government reported financial transactions on a modified accrual basis and all fixed assets (including real property) were reported at a $1.00 nominal value in the government balance sheet, the statement of assets and liabilities. In effect, real property was treated as an expenditure at the time it was acquired, and ultimately as a source of cash at the time it was disposed of. As the federal government is a major holder of real property, this approach did not reflect the federal government's related accountabilities and responsibilities. This approach also understated the true strategic significance of real property within the federal government, both in terms of 'store of value' and 'value in use'.

The decision to move to accrual accounting has had a profound effect on how the government manages its assets, including real property assets. As Canada is one of the largest countries in the world in terms of land mass, the federal government owns a considerable amount of real property, so the task of identifying all of this and accounting for it, and then managing it accordingly and in the context of sustainable development, was and continues to be a considerable challenge.

Since 1995 the Government of Canada has undertaken many initiatives to greatly improve the management of its real property assets. These have included extensive consultation and collaboration with people and organisations, both inside and outside the federal government, and the development of associated policies, guidelines and inventories.

Management of Real Property

The federal government's Real Property Management Framework Policy provides the overall policy in this area. It is government policy to acquire, manage and retain real property only to support the delivery of government programmes and to do so in a manner consistent with the principle of sustainable development. Accordingly, when managing real property, departments and agencies must do so in a manner that will preserve the maximum long-term economic advantage to the Crown; honour federal environmental objectives; provide safe and adequate facilities; and respect other relevant government policies.

In support of this policy, the federal government designed and developed a web-based federal real property database that contains common real property data for over 20,000 owned and leased properties for 85 custodian organisations.

This *Directory of Federal Real Property* is now the central record and only complete listing of real property holdings of the Government of Canada and includes basic information concerning federal real property such as custodian identification, property size, location and type of legal interest. The directory, which is administered by the TBS, maintains a contemporary record of basic information concerning the government's real property holdings, and is used to keep the government informed about the scale and major components of its real property inventory. It is also used to provide information to ministers, Members of Parliament and the general public concerning a specific property or group of properties within a particular geographic area.

Although all Crown lands in Canada are owned by Her Majesty the Queen, their administration is assigned to departments, agencies and Crown corporations to support the delivery of government programmes. These organisations are commonly referred to as custodians.

Management of Contaminated Sites

To strengthen its management of contaminated sites, the Government of Canada issued its Federal Contaminated Sites and Solid Waste Landfills Inventory Policy on 1 July 1 2000 to require departments and agencies that hold property to establish and maintain a database of their contaminated sites and solid waste landfills, and to submit this to the TBS for inclusion in a central inventory database. This inventory, which is linked to the *Directory* mentioned above, includes all known federal contaminated sites for which departments and agencies are accountable. It does not include properties owned by Crown corporations. Sites vary from several square metres of soil contaminated by leaking batteries to abandoned mine sites in the North contaminated with heavy metals. The inventory also includes non-federal contaminated sites for which the Government of Canada has accepted some, or all, financial responsibility.

The inventory project began in June 2000 when the government committed itself to gather and make public a list of its contaminated sites. To achieve this, the government allocated a total of $30 million to assist departments in assessing, identifying and classifying their sites. With much of the assessment and identification work completed, the government is now fulfilling its commitment to openness and transparency by making the inventory of federal sites available to all Canadians. The inventory is very much 'work in progress', to which additional sites and improved information will continually be added.

The classification system used in the inventory was developed by the Canadian Council of Ministers of the Environment (CCME). Under this system, a permanent classification is assigned to each site at the time it is assessed for contaminants, sites for which action is required being listed as Class 1, and sites for which action is likely to be required as Class 2, etc. It is important to note that the initial classification of a site will not change, no matter what steps are taken to remediate or otherwise manage the site. This means that even in situations where Class 1 sites have already been remediated, they will still retain their standing as Class 1 sites. However, their 'current status' would change to 'remediation completed'.

The inventory includes key information such as:

• Description and number of sites;

• The current status of each contaminated site;

• The percentage formed by each of the following categories: under assessment, under remediation, remediated and under risk management, under risk management, remediation complete and assessed with no action required.

The inventory also includes information by class for each department and for each region or territory.

Having had sufficient time to input information into the inventory and after extensive consultations, the federal government promulgated its Contaminated Sites Management Policy in 2002. The policy provides for consistent management of federal contaminated sites in support of sound stewardship of federal real property assets through the systematic identification and categorisation of risks, the development of management plans with an early focus on reducing the risks to human health, safety or the environment, optimal use of financial and technological resources through the use of a risk management approach; and the development of innovative strategies to recover the social and economic value of federal contaminated sites.

Four major organisations have responsibilities under the new policy.

Custodian departments and agencies are responsible for the management of federal contaminated sites under their administration and discharge their responsibilities in a manner consistent with their interest in the real property and with the management framework for the property. The TBS is responsible for the establishment and maintenance of the Contaminated Sites Management Framework and the provision of strategic policy advice. Public Works and Government Services Canada, as a common services provider, is available to provide technical and management services to support government departments in implementing their contaminated sites management responsibilities on a cost-recovery basis. Environment Canada plays a leadership role by providing specialist advice and guidance to government departments, agencies, stakeholders and other interest groups on the application and interpretation of federal and provincial policies, guidelines and programmes that may relate to federal contaminated sites; promotes compliance with regulatory requirements and guidance; serves as a liaison with provincial and territorial governments; and develops, in co-operation with partners, environmental quality criteria, site assessment protocols and remediation technologies.

Identifying Contaminated Sites

According to the definition adopted by the government, a contaminated site is 'one at which substances occur at concentrations (1) above (normally occurring) background levels and pose or are likely to pose an immediate or long-term hazard to human health or the environment or (2) exceeding levels specified in policies and regulations'.

The main qualification for including a site in the inventory is that there is a concentration of a substance in the soil or ground water (usually a petroleum product or a metal) that is higher than expected for that region of Canada. There must also be some evidence that this concentration poses a risk to human health or the environment.

This risk is determined in a step-by-step process, beginning with a rough estimate of the contamination based on guidelines agreed to by federal, provincial and territorial environment ministers, all of whom are members of the Canadian Council of Ministers of the Environment. The final stage in the procedure process is an Environmental Site Assessment that uses such tools as field sampling and laboratory analysis to determine the type and level of contamination present.

Although the inventory does not currently contain any solid waste landfills, these areas are defined as 'sites that have been subject to engineered waste control mechanisms which may include soil filling or covering, hydrogeological monitoring, or management of the waste disposal process'. A solid waste landfill may or may not be a contaminated site.

Accounting for Contaminated Sites

At the same time, the federal government issued its policy on Accounting for Costs and Liabilities Related to Contaminated Sites to ensure that all costs and liabilities related to the management and remediation of environmentally contaminated sites, for which the Government of Canada has ongoing responsibility, are accounted for and reported in the financial statements of the government in the fiscal year in which environmental damage is incurred, or in the fiscal year in which costs and liabilities are identified.

Supporting Material

Real Property Management
http://www.tbs-sct.gc.ca/rpm-gbi/home-accueil.asp?Language=EN

Federal Contaminated Sites Management Policy
http://www.tbs-sct.gc.ca/pubs_pol/dcgpubs/realproperty/fcsmp-gscf_e.asp

Policy on Accounting for Costs and Liabilities Related to Contaminated Sites
http://www.tbs-sct.gc.ca/Pubs_pol/dcgpubs/TBM_142/aclcs-ccpsc_e.html

Commissioner of the Environment and Sustainable Development
http://www.oag-bvg.gc.ca/domino/oag-bvg.nsf/html/environment.html)

5 The Policy-making Process

5.1 Institutional Arrangements for Policy Development

The Cabinet Decision-Making System

While the executive functions of Canada's parliamentary system of responsible government are vested in the Crown by the Canadian Constitution, in practice these functions are carried out by the Prime Minister and the Cabinet, as long as they enjoy the confidence of Parliament. The Prime Minister and the Cabinet, two fundamental institutions of parliamentary government, are not defined in either the formal constitution or in law.

The formation of the Ministry and the structure of Cabinet decision-making are among the Prime Minister's most important prerogatives. However, not all members of the Ministry are members of the Cabinet; as of May 2003 there are 28 Cabinet ministers (including the Prime Minister) and ten Secretaries of State. The position of Secretary of State was created in November 1993, to provide additional support to Cabinet ministers and the government in meeting the objectives set out by the Prime Minister.

Cabinet decision-making is led by certain key statements on government policy and priorities; the Speech from the Throne provides the government with a policy framework, and the budget exercise, culminating in the tabling of the Estimates, establishes the fiscal framework. These frameworks provide for the overall direction of the government and shape the work of Cabinet committees.

In the long-standing tradition of Cabinet government, only ministers attend meetings of the Cabinet and its committees. Secretaries of State are sworn as Privy Councillors, as are ministers, and may be invited to accompany their portfolio minister to a Cabinet or Cabinet committee

120

meeting. Parliamentary Secretaries may not do so as they are not members of the Ministry and are not sworn to the Privy Council. The Prime Minister decides whether exceptions are to be made to these conventions. The Secretary to the Cabinet attends Cabinet meetings and other officials attend as required.

Generally, Cabinet business consists of proposed actions aimed at implementing the government's agenda, items of special urgency, parliamentary business, political issues, the review of senior appointments and any other matter of general concern to Canadians or the government.

Issues are normally introduced by a Memorandum to Cabinet prepared by a minister, which is tendered to the appropriate Cabinet committee after it has been circulated to all ministers. The Prime Minister expects issues to be dealt with at the committee stage. Cabinet is not used to air introductory or preliminary factors relating to the issue at hand. It is the deputy minister's responsibility to ensure that affected departments are adequately informed in advance of the issues before Cabinet. In other words, the bulk of collective ministerial deliberations take place in committee; Cabinet committee recommendations are subject to confirmation by Cabinet. This allows Cabinet to concentrate on priority issues, as well as on broad policy and political concerns. Ministers are not asked to vote on the various items; once discussion has taken place and ministers have expressed their views, the Prime Minister calls the consensus. Once a decision has been reached, it is recorded and communicated throughout the government.

Cabinet Committee Structure

Cabinet committees are an extension of the Cabinet itself. As First Minister, it is the Prime Minister's prerogative to organise Cabinet and the Cabinet committee decision-making system, establish the agenda for Cabinet meetings and designate committee chairpersons to act on his on her behalf. Currently, most collective ministerial deliberations take place in Cabinet committees. Committee chairpersons act for the Prime Minister with his or her authority, including setting committee agenda. For the most part, decisions are taken by the appropriate committee, subject to confirmation by the Cabinet. Currently, there are five Cabinet committees:

- The Cabinet Committee for the Economic Union (20 members);

- The Cabinet Committee for the Social Union (18 members);
- The Special Committee of Council (9 members);
- The Treasury Board (six members and six alternates);
- The Cabinet Committee on Government Communications (16 members).

The first two committees deal with economic and social policy issues, respectively. The Special Committee of Council (SCC) exercises legislative authority that is conferred on the Governor in Council. In practice the SCC, acting on behalf of Cabinet, is responsible for reviewing and making recommendations to the Governor General. The Treasury Board is the only Cabinet committee established by law and many of its decisions have force of law. The Treasury Board is the employer of the public service, and establishes policies and common standards for administrative, personnel, financial and organisational functions across government. It also controls the allocation of financial resources to departments and programmes. Finally, the Cabinet Committee on Government Communications has a mandate to review the government's communications strategy and approve key communications activities.

The Prime Minister may also choose to constitute ad hoc Cabinet committees whenever it is necessary. For instance, the Ad Hoc Cabinet Committee on Public Safety and Anti-Terrorism was established after the events of 11 September 2001. The committee is comprised of the ministers involved in Canada's response to terrorism threats and in the protection of Canada and Canadians; it is chaired by the Deputy Prime Minister.

Privy Council Office
The primary responsibility of the Privy Council Office is to provide public service support to the Prime Minister, ministers within the Prime Minister's portfolio and the Cabinet in order to facilitate the smooth and effective operation of the Government of Canada.

The PCO is the public service department of the Prime Minister. Under the leadership of the Clerk of the Privy Council and Secretary to the Cabinet, the PCO provides direct support to the Prime Minister across the range of functions and responsibilities of the head of government.

The key responsibility of the Clerk of the Privy Council and Secretary to the Cabinet is to provide direct support to the Prime Minister from the perspective of the values, traditions and expertise of the Public Service of Canada. In that context, the Clerk plays three interrelated roles:

- He serves as the Prime Minister's Deputy Minister;

- He is the Secretary to the Cabinet;

- He is the Head of the Public Service of Canada.

As the Prime Minister's Deputy Minister, the Clerk provides advice and support to the Prime Minister in areas that are of special concern to his role as head of government. The Prime Minister looks to the Clerk of the Privy Council for advice in operating the Cabinet decision-making system, in setting overall policy direction, in enhancing intergovernmental relations, in appointing senior office holders and organising the government, and in managing specific issues.

As Secretary to the Cabinet, the Clerk of the Privy Council assists the Prime Minister to maintain the cohesion of the Ministry and give direction to it. In this role, the incumbent provides support and advice to the Ministry as a whole to ensure that the Cabinet decision-making system operates effectively and efficiently according to the design of the Prime Minister.

As Head of the Public Service, the Clerk serves as the main link between the Prime Minister and the federal public service, and is responsible to the Prime Minister for the institution's overall performance and its effective management.

The Privy Council Office provides advice and support to the Prime Minister in carrying out his or her functions in the following areas:

- Appointments;

- Mandates and government organisation;

- Government's relations with Parliament and the Crown;

- Cabinet and Cabinet committees organisation and operations;

- Government policy directions;

- Leadership and direction to the government;

- Constitutional responsibilities, including those relating to the Governor General;

- Foreign affairs and national security;

- Intergovernmental affairs.

In addition, the Privy Council Office supports the Clerk of the Privy Council and Secretary to the Cabinet as Head of the Public Service. In this capacity, the Clerk has the combined responsibility both for the overall effectiveness of the Public Service and for its competent and efficient management and administration.

Prime Minister's Office

The Prime Minister is supported directly by two organisations within his portfolio. The Prime Minister's Office is comprised of the Prime Minister's personal and political staff. The PCO serves as the Prime Minister's public service department and as secretariat to the Cabinet and its committees. While these two organisations differ greatly in their respective roles and mandates, they are sensitive to the need for consultation and co-ordination in their efforts to serve the Prime Minister and the Cabinet.

The precise role of the Prime Minister's Office varies according to the personal style and preferences of the Prime Minister in office, and its organisation is left entirely to his or her discretion. The present Prime Minister's Office, under the direction of the Chief of Staff, is composed of politically-oriented staff members; they are not public servants.

The Prime Minister's Office provides advice and support to the Prime Minister, as leader of the political party forming the government, on priorities, political strategy and tactics, and the political dimensions of policy initiatives. It is organised to ensure national political liaison with ministers, caucus and the party in general. The Prime Minister's Office supports the Prime Minister in his role as a Member of Parliament and handles all constituency matters. A team of advisers is also responsible for briefing the Prime Minister on the main affairs concerning the development of Canadian society and the international community.

The support functions of the Prime Minister's Office include co-ordinating the Prime Minister's agenda and travel, managing his or her communications, including speeches, and preparing correspondence.

Supporting Material

Privy Council Office website
www.pco-bcp.gc.ca

Selected Privy Council Office documents available on the Privy Council
Office website under 'Publications':
    Cabinet Directive on Law-Making (2003)
    Guide to Making Federal Acts and Regulations (2003)
    Decision-Making Processes and Central Agencies in Canada; Federal,
    Provincial and Territorial Practices (1998)
    A Guide for Ministers and Secretaries of State (2002)
    Memoranda to Cabinet: a Drafter's Guide (2000)

PCO's Regulatory Affairs and Order in Council Secretariat's website
www.pco-bcp.gc.ca/raoics/srdc/

5.2 Roles and Responsibilities in Policy Management

The Prime Minister is the authoritative spokesperson on the policy of
the government. The Prime Minister is responsible to Parliament for
the overall spending programme of the government, which ultimately
reflects how the priorities, policies and programmes of the Ministry are
defined and implemented, and leads the process of setting the general
direction of government policy.

The development of government policy is a complex and continuing
process. Ministers identify and propose priorities and initiatives on the
basis of their portfolio and other responsibilities. Certain individual
ministers exercise special co-ordinating functions on behalf of the
Ministry as a whole. Under the direction of the Prime Minister, policy
proposals are evaluated and combined to form an overall agenda which
has the support of the entire Ministry.

The Privy Council Office provides advice to the Prime Minister on
the overall conduct of government business, including the strategic
handling of major issues and subjects that are of particular interest
to the Prime Minister. The objective is to ensure that all the affected
interests have been consulted, and that a full range of alternatives has
been considered prior to decisions – in sum, that the Prime Minister
and the Cabinet possess the information required to make decisions.

In this context, a key function of the Privy Council Office is the co-ordination of policy to ensure complementarity among new proposals, existing policies and the government's overall priorities and objectives. The PCO works closely with the Prime Minister's Office, the Department of Finance, the TBS and other agencies and departments to provide ministers with comprehensive briefings on the issues before them for decisions and, after decisions are made, to disseminate the information and arrange for the follow-up measures required for effective implementation. The participation of the PCO in policy development and implementation is an integral part of its central role in supporting the Prime Minister to ensure the effective operation of the government.

5.3 Reform of the Policy Development Process

The Prime Minister has not undertaken major changes to the Cabinet decision-making process since Canada's last country profile was published in 1995. However, the Prime Minister has made some adjustments that are worth mentioning.

In 1997, as part of changes to the Cabinet decision-making system, he authorised changes to the mandate of the Special Committee of Council (SCC). The SCC was tasked with new responsibilities to oversee legislative issues and planning, in addition to considering and approving submissions to the Governor in Council and regulations made pursuant to statutory authority. The Prime Minister also decided to give SCC the mandate to serve as policy committee to review issues of legislative policy and process, and for issues concerning electoral reform. PCO provides all necessary support to the work of the Special Committee of Council.

In January 2001, the Cabinet Committee on Government Com-munications was established as the fifth standing committee and was given the mandate to co-ordinate the overall government com-munications strategy and implementation, and to ensure the consistency and effectiveness of the communications function.

In 1999, a Cabinet Directive was issued which sets out the objectives and expectations of the Cabinet in relation to the government's law-making activities. Departmental officials involved in these activities are expected to follow the instructions it contains. The main objectives of the Directive are to:

- Ensure that the Cabinet has the information and other support it needs to make sound decisions about proposed laws;

- Outline the relationship between Acts and regulations and ensure that they are viewed as products of a continuous process of law-making;

- Ensure that proposed laws are properly drafted in both official languages and that they respect both the common and civil law legal systems;

- Make it clear that law-making initiatives can be very complex and must be properly planned and managed;

- Ensure that government officials who are involved in law-making activities understand their roles and have the knowledge and skills needed to perform their duties effectively.

In addition to the Cabinet Directive on Law-Making, a second edition of the *Guide to Making Federal Acts and Regulations* was released in February 2003. The guide provides detailed information on various aspects of the legislative process.

In 2000, the Prime Minister approved the creation of the first 'reference group' of ministers. Reference groups of ministers are created in order to conduct in-depth analysis of a policy issue and for ministers to arrive at a common understanding of that issue. Meetings of the reference groups are not formal Cabinet meetings and have no decision-making authority.

5.4 New Initiatives Intended at Strengthening Policy-Making

The Policy Research Initiative

The Policy Research Initiative (PRI) was established in 1996 to strengthen the government's ability to identify, understand and address medium and longer-term cross-cutting policy research issues.

The PRI's mandate is articulated around three main goals:

- To enhance, collect and integrate research work on emerging horizontal issues and better integrate it into the medium-term policy agenda of the federal government;

- To contribute to the strengthening of the federal government's capacity to develop and maintain a vibrant policy research community;

- To create an infrastructure to support horizontal policy research collaboration.

The PRI staff are responsible for the development and execution of research projects in partnerships with government departments. Small research teams are set up for each project, acting as hubs for larger teams of experts and analysts from participating departments. The work plans and timelines for the projects are organised in such a way as to be responsive to the cycle of policy and planning activities of the government.

The capacity-building objective is mainly dealt with through the Policy Research Development Program (PRDP). The aim of the PRDP is to bring into government highly qualified graduate students who have specialised in policy research. The programme, which is managed by the PRI, makes available ten policy research development positions in departments across government.

Improving the policy research potential in lower-capacity departments is also a basic requirement of the capacity-building objective. Thus, departments with limited policy research capacity, or which are trying to create such capacity, should be among the beneficiaries of the PRDP programme.

Finally, the infrastructure-building objective is being met by a number of vehicles. The PRI delivers a variety of regional and national, multidisciplinary, policy research conferences and seminars. The PRI also chairs the Policy Research Data Group (PRDG), an interdepartmental committee that manages a fund for the development of data products and services in support of emerging horizontal policy issues.

Two deputy ministers oversee the overall strategic direction of the PRI and work in close collaboration with the PRI's Executive Director, who is responsible for the general direction of research projects and activities. The PRI occasionally reports to the Co-ordinating Committee of Deputy Ministers, and many of its projects and programmes are guided by advisory committees made up of government senior officials.

Communications and Consultations

Consultation and citizen engagement processes invite greater citizen involvement in the development of government policies, programmes and services. The involvement of citizens in dialogue on public policy issues is an integral part of the Canadian democratic system. Like other democratic governments around the world, the Government of Canada has recently begun to explore on-line participatory approaches.

Traditionally, citizens' views have been reflected in the policy-making process through three avenues:

- Members of Parliament, who represent the views of their constituents in the House of Commons and House committees, and liaise with citizens through newsletters, websites and informal meetings in their constituencies;

- Voluntary organisations and stakeholder groups, which provide a focal point for civic discourse, representing the views of their members and, in some cases, of a broader range of citizens on public policy issues; and

- Government consultation and citizen engagement processes, which are undertaken by departments and agencies at the request of ministers, and are designed to complement – not replace – the previous two avenues of public involvement.

While these channels remain effective vehicles for reflecting the views of Canadian citizens, new information technologies, such as the internet, are providing further opportunities to enhance public involvement and are changing the relationship between governments and citizens.

On-line participation in the Government of Canada is grounded in a governance context, with technology viewed as an enabler. In this context, the emphasis is on the application of sound public participation principles and practices, rather than on the technology. In most cases, both on-line and off-line approaches are integrated in a complementary manner.

On-line participatory approaches have obvious advantages for reaching citizens in rural or isolated areas and for engaging specific target populations, such as youth, who may not participate in more traditional consultative approaches. They also offer flexibility. Those who may not have time to attend a town hall meeting or participate in a public dialogue session can access the internet, review a discussion paper and provide comments at their convenience.

In spite of the obvious advantages of on-line participation, there are also limitations and challenges. Public awareness of on-line consultations and access to the internet are major issues, as are security and privacy concerns. In addition, not all public engagement processes lend themselves to an on-line environment. For example, deliberative dialogue techniques are often more effective conducted in a face-to-face context.

Like many advanced economies, Canada is addressing the digital divide, specifically through its 'Connecting Canadians' initiative, as well as through measures to bring broadband access to the Canadian public over the next few years. The government is also working to establish a secure infrastructure for government-citizen interactions on-line through its Government On-Line Initiative.

The Canadian Government is still in the early stages of developing on-line participation tools and techniques. All departments now have an internet presence and many are currently exploring on-line approaches as a complement to more traditional forms of consultation and engagement.

The Privy Council Office, in collaboration with others, provides support to both on-line and off-line consultation and citizen engagement processes. An overarching e-participation strategy is currently being developed, involving policy, research, infrastructure and capacity-building elements.

The PCO has already started to document early experiences with on-line consultation, both within the Canadian Government and internationally, so that lessons can be shared and appropriate support provided.

In an effort to build capacity for on-line consultation and engagement within the government, the PCO and the TBS have prepared draft 'Guidelines for On-line Consultation and Citizen Engagement'. The PCO also organises monthly e-learning seminars and has established an on-line consultation website which contains reference material and examples of best practice. It is currently liaising with the Canadian Centre for Management Development to develop a range of e-consultation learning opportunities for government officials with responsibilities or an interest in this area.

In addition to these internal activities, the Government of Canada collaborates with Canadian academic, not-for-profit and private sector organisations and internationally with the OECD, the European Commission, the UK and other leading governments, fostering an exchange of ideas and experiences both at home and abroad.

Supporting Material

Policy Research Initiative
www.policyresearch.gc.ca

5.5 Recent Developments in the Management of Key Policy Issues

Aboriginals Policy

The resolution of claims and the move towards self-government agreements with First Nations has continued to be a priority in the last decade. In addition, there have been significant efforts to better understand the complex challenges facing Aboriginal people and to develop policy approaches to meet those challenges.

In 1991, a Royal Commission on Aboriginal People (RCAP) was struck, and its final report, tabled in 1996, provided an important body of research to inform policy development. The federal government response to RCAP, *Gathering Strength*, was an action plan intended to begin to address the needs of Aboriginal people, and subsequent policy initiatives have built on this framework.

Since 1993, a cornerstone of Canada's Aboriginal policy has been the recognition of their inherent right of self-government under section 35 of the Canadian Constitution. Following consultations on this proposed approach, the federal policy framework to implement this inherent right was launched in 1995.

The federal approach to Aboriginal self-government, based on negotiation, will result in new arrangements to give Aboriginal communities the tools they need to exercise greater control over their lives. Self-government arrangements will recognise the right of Aboriginal peoples to make decisions about matters internal to their communities, integral to their unique cultures, traditions and languages, and connected with their relationship to the land and resources.

Under federal policy, Aboriginal groups may negotiate self-government arrangements in a variety of areas, including government structure, land management, health care, child welfare, education, housing and economic development. Negotiations will be between Aboriginal groups, the federal government and, in areas affecting its jurisdiction and interests, the relevant provincial or territorial government.

The federal government has recently introduced the proposed *First Nations Government Act*. When it becomes law, the Act will provide governance tools to bands operating under the *Indian Act* in matters of leadership selection, administration of government, financial management and accountability, legal capacity and law making.

Canada is also taking steps to ensure that the institutional framework is in place to provide First Nations with the economic levers ordinarily available to governments. Legislation currently before the House of Commons will lead to the creation of the First Nations Tax Commission, First Nations Financial Management Board, First Nations Finance Authority and First Nations Statistical Institute.

These legislative initiatives serve to provide First Nations with more tools to assist them in moving towards self-government.

Intergovernmental Affairs Policy
Federalism is a structure of government that offers the benefits of political and economic union combined with local autonomy. Canada has such a system, with legislative powers distributed between a national government and the provinces.

The division of powers between the federal government and provincial governments was set out in the *Constitution Act, 1867*, particularly in sections 91 and 92. The federal Parliament was given jurisdiction over matters considered national in scope, such as protecting the federation from military threats and 'trade and commerce', promoting economic growth and development. The provinces were given responsibility for areas considered to be of more local concern, such as hospitals and education, which are important in maintaining their specific identities, cultures and special institutions. The residual power refers to all powers not specifically assigned to either jurisdiction; it was assigned to the federal government. Several formal changes have been made to the original division of jurisdiction.

Fiscal federalism

The capacity of the federal, provincial and territorial governments to assume their responsibilities centres on the balance between decentralisation of revenues and decentralisation of government spending, the scale of transfers between orders of government, the conditions attached to those transfers, the differences in the respective capacity of the provinces and territories to provide comparable public services at comparable levels of taxation, and tax collection arrangements within the country.

One of the most important aspects of Canadian federalism is determined by the need to transfer money to provincial governments to fund the programmes for which they are constitutionally responsible. The Government of Canada does this in two ways:

- The first method consists of making equalisation payments, which are provided to the poorer provinces in order to compensate for their smaller revenue base;

- The second method is via programme payments paid by the federal government to all provinces to fund programmes it considers important.

Provincial economies vary greatly in their respective economic strengths and taxation capacity. Consequently, the federal government makes equalisation payments to the poorer provinces to enable them to provide reasonable comparable levels of public services at reasonable comparable levels of taxation (a provision set out in section 36.2 of the 1982 *Constitution Act*).

The Canada Health and Social Transfer (CHST) is the main vehicle by which the federal government assists all provincial governments to finance provincial health, education and welfare programmes. Federal spending power allows the federal government to make expenditures in policy areas that are normally under provincial jurisdiction.

The Landscape

In recent years, the focus of intergovernmental affairs has shifted away from large-scale constitutional reform to clarifying the roles of the federal and provincial governments within the current constitutional framework.

There has been considerable co-ordination of policy advances, brought about through intergovernmental negotiations among first ministers and ministers responsible for particular policy areas, as well as among federal and provincial officials.

The Government of Canada has taken certain measures to respond to the requests and changing priorities, including:

- Withdrawal of the federal government from the areas of labour market training, mining and forest development, recreation, tourism and the administration of social housing;

- Major joint federal-provincial initiatives such as the National Child Benefit, homelessness, and the 2000 Accords on health and early childhood development;

- Adoption of the Social Union Framework agreement, intended to guide governments in developing and reviewing social policies and programmes and in managing their interdependence more effectively.

Supporting Material

Aboriginals Policy
www. ainc-inac.gc.ca

Intergovernmental Affairs Policy
www.pco-bcp.gc.ca/aia/

Conclusion: Looking Forward

The preceding pages present an impressive number and wide scope of reforms that have occurred during the eight or more years since the first edition of this profile. This in no way means that reform will now come to an end or even slow down.

As we look forward in 2003 and try to identify future challenges, the emerging priorities of the government's management board provide some clues to the broad and significant issues that will need to be tackled. The Treasury Board Secretariat has been pursuing an already substantial agenda of 'management change' and much of this will continue to be pursued in the coming fiscal year and beyond in all three business lines – stewardship, human resources and service improvement. It is also considering the development of an integrated management framework to inform and guide its new approach to relations with departments and agencies, and to provide an accountability framework offering greater clarity on the division of accountabilities between the Treasury Board and departments and agencies, as well as setting clear performance expectations. Strengthening integrity, accountability, and values and ethics could also involve revision of the public service conflict of interest and post-employment guidelines, and the publication of a code of public service values and ethics.

The introduction in February 2003 of human resources reform legislation to modernise the legislative framework for human resources management in the public service (Bill C-25) is expected to bring about the most significant change to the public service legislative framework in nearly four decades. If adopted, it will mean changes to a number of statutes in the areas of staffing, recourse, relations between labour and management and learning, and institutional changes affecting the Public Service Commission, the Canadian Centre for Management

Development and the TBS. Implementation will take several years because of the need to draft regulations and policies to support it; negotiate and implement transfers of responsibilities and resources; establish new organisations and staff them; and train the HR community, as well as staff and managers, in the new system. There will also be non-legislative HR reforms, for example advances on the Embracing Change Report commitments to diversify the public service so that it better reflects the demographic realities of the country and to improve performance on other employment equity groups in the public service; to implement the new Official Languages Plan; to expand public service learning activity and programmes through the development of a standard entry level orientation programming, mandatory programming for different levels of responsibility or functional responsibilities and increasing knowledge transfer capacity; and to further advance the work on leadership development, including the establishment of a broader and deeper leadership continuum and collective management of assistant deputy ministers.

In the area of stewardship, the Modern Comptrollership Initiative has been extended to 88 departments and agencies from the original five pilot departments. It will focus on strengthening and improving performance on all fronts in all organisations and it continues to be a corporate priority for the Clerk of the Privy Council (who is also Head of the Public Service). Improved reporting to Parliament and the public (i.e. providing more 'whole-of-government' reporting, reducing the number of reports and consolidating all existing Treasury Board reports on the Public Service) and the move to accrual accounting will also create challenges. Attention will also focus on the new five-year cycle of expenditure and management reviews on non-statutory spending (both 'vertical', i.e. department or agency specific, and 'horizontal', i.e. policies and programmes that cut across departments and agencies); the need to reduce the non-statutory A base in FY 2003–2004 by $1 billion; and the need to consult with Parliament and the Auditor General on changes to government reporting to Parliament.

Finally, with regard to service improvement, the Canadian Government is committed to have all key services on-line and to achieve a 10 per cent improvement in Canadians' satisfaction with the delivery of key government services by 2005. Several other service improvement initiatives are being envisaged: a move towards greater service integration within government; development of an integrated single window employee portal; approval of a management of government information policy; and the elaboration of government IT security standards.

At the beginning of the new century, it is obvious that reforms will be continuous. The challenge is to formulate a coherent and integrated management framework for the Canadian public service, one that will ensure that governance goals are met, that the focus is on results and that accountability is strong throughout the system.

While this profile will help readers to catch up on Canadian reforms, they will obviously need to follow closely the continuing evolution of the Canadian model, as major developments are continuing or beginning in many areas such as citizen engagement, an ethics and integrity package, human resource management, excellence in management, electronic government, continuous learning, official languages and many more areas. Readers should continue visiting the appropriate websites for recent updates.

A new goal was set for the Canadian public service by the Clerk of the Privy Council in the *10th Annual Report of the Head of the Public Service* in April 2003: 'We can justifiably aspire to setting the world standard for a professional public service'. Future updates of this profile thus promise to be even more full of discoveries than this one. They should reveal an even more mature and more sophisticated model of management excellence.

Further Reading

Links to some Key Government and Organisation Websites

Main site: Government of Canada
http://www.canada.gc.ca
This is the Government of Canada primary internet site, providing general information about Canada and links to Canadian government information and services.

Central Agencies:
Privy Council Office
http://www.pco-bcp.gc.ca

Department of Finance
http://www.fin.gc.ca

Treasury Board Secretariat
http://www.tbs-sct.gc.ca
Provides links to the key policies and publications concerning the human, financial, information and technology resource management of the Canadian government.

Public Service Commission
http://www.psc-cfp.gc.ca
General information on public service human resource management

Regulatory Affairs and Orders in Council Secretariat
http://www.pco-bcp.gc.ca/raoics-srdc/

Policy Research Initiative
http://www.policyresearch.gc.ca

Canadian Centre for Management Development
http://www.ccmd-ccg.gc.ca
For information about trends in executive learning, including information about executive education and development programmes and
services and access to documents. Also provides numerous research
publications, including the Deputy Minister Task Force Reports and
recent action-research reports.

The Leadership Network and *La Relève*
http://www.leadership.gc.ca

The Institute of Public Administration of Canada
http://www.ipaciapc.ca/english/menu.htm

The Institute for Citizen-Centred Service
http://www.iccs-isac.org/eng/

Key Documents on Public Management Issues and Developments in Canada

For more detailed background and/or analytical perspectives on Canada and its reforms of this period see:

Bourgault, J., Demers, M. and Williams, C. (eds), *Public Administration and Public Management: Canadian Experiences*, Les Publications du Québec, Sainte-Foy, 1997, 418 pp. (also available in French).

Bouckaert, Geert and Pollitt, Christopher, *Public Management Reform: A Comparative Analysis*, Oxford University Press, 314 pp. This comparative study of ten countries includes a section on Canada, pp. 208–217.

Bourgon, Jocelyne, 'The Public Sector in the Knowledge Age – The Canadian Experience: Challenges and Opportunities', speech at the CCMD Conference on Changing Governance and Public Sector Reform in the Americas, Ottawa, 2 May 2001.

OECD, *OECD Praises Canada's Regulatory Reforms and Encourages Sustained Momentum*, 2002 *http://www.oecd.org/EN/document/0,,EN-document-0-nodirectorate-no-12-36057-0,00.html*

OECD, *Issues and Developments in Public Management, Canada*, 2001 http://www.oecd.org/pdf/M00006000/M00006250.pdf

Annex A offers a table of Principal Recent Public Management Developments 1995–2001.

Annex B explains the major roles of key agencies: Institutional Responsibility for Public Management Improvement.

For other key documents of this period, see:

Service Improvement

Citizens First 3, Institute for Citizen-Centred Service, Toronto, March 2003 *http://iccs-isac.org/eng/cf-02.htm*

Citizens First, The Citizen-Centred Service Network, Canadian Centre for Management Development, 1998, Ottawa.

Common Services Policy, Treasury Board of Canada Secretariat, 1997, Ottawa.

Strategic Directions for Information Management and Information Technology: Enabling 21st Century Service to Canadians, Treasury Board Secretariat, 1999, Ottawa.

The Enhanced Management Framework for Information Management and Information Technology 'Solutions: Putting the Principles to Work', Treasury Board Secretariat, 1999, Ottawa.

Stewardship

Results for Canadians: A Management Framework for the Government of Canada, Treasury Board Secretariat, 2000, Ottawa *http://www.tbs-sct.gc.ca/res_can/rc_e.asp*

Managing for Results, Treasury Board Secretariat, 1999, Ottawa.

Treasury Board and Business Planning Principles, Treasury Board Secretariat, 1999, Ottawa.

Accounting for Results: Annual Report to Parliament by the President of the Treasury Board, President of the Treasury Board, Minister of Supply and Services, 1997, Ottawa.

Assessment Framework for Modernizing Comptrollership, Treasury Board Secretariat, 1998, Ottawa.

Financial Information Strategy Learning Framework, Treasury Board Secretariat, 1999, Ottawa.

Getting Government Right: Governing for Canadians, Treasury Board of Canada Secretariat, 1997, Ottawa.

Cost Recovery and Charging Policy, Treasury Board of Canada Secretariat, 1997, Ottawa.

Getting Government Right: Improving Results Measurement and Accountability: Annual Report to Parliament by the President of the Treasury Board, President of the Treasury Board, Minister of Supply and Services, 1996, Ottawa.

Improved Reporting to Parliament Project: Departmental Performance Reports and Reports on Plans and Priorities, Treasury Board of Canada Secretariat, Ottawa.

Report of the Independent Review Panel on Modernization of Comptrollership in the Government of Canada, Treasury Board of Canada Secretariat, Minister of Supply and Services, 1997, Ottawa.

The Expenditure Management System of the Government of Canada, Treasury Board of Canada Secretariat, Minister of Supply and Services, 1995, Ottawa.

User Charging in the Federal Government: A Background Document, Treasury Board of Canada Secretariat, 1996, Ottawa.

Human Resource Management

First Progress Report on La Relève: A Commitment to Action, La Relève Task Force, Privy Council Office, 1998, Ottawa.

Framework for Good Human Resources Management in the Public Service, Treasury Board Secretariat, 1999, Ottawa.

Recruitment and Results: Report of the COSO Sub-Committee on Recruitment, Privy Council Office, 2000, Ottawa.

Update for HR Professionals on Business Planning and Reporting in the Government of Canada, Treasury Board Secretariat, 1999, Ottawa.

Workplace Well-being – The Challenge: Report of the COSO Sub-Committee on Workplace Well-being, Privy Council Office, 2000, Ottawa.

Action Plan for Official Languages, March 2003
http//www.pco-bcp.gc.ca/aia/default.asp?Language=E&page=actionplan&doc=action plan_e.htm

Policy-Making and Public Service

Annual Reports to the Prime Minister on The Public Service of Canada, Privy Council Office, Clerk of the Privy Council (1992, then yearly from 1994), Ottawa
http://www.pco-bcp.gc.ca/default.asp?Language=E&Page=clerk&Sub=AnnualReports

A Strong Foundation – Report of the Task Force on Public Service Values and Ethics, Canadian Centre for Management and Development, 1996, Ottawa.

Deputy Minister Task Forces:

Report of the Deputy Minister Task Force on Service Delivery Models, Privy Council Office, 1996, Ottawa.

Report of the Deputy Minister Task Force on Strengthening Policy Capacity, Privy Council Office, 1996, Ottawa.

Report of the Deputy Minister Task Force on Managing Horizontal Policy Issues, Privy Council Office, 1996, Ottawa.

Report of the Deputy Minister Task Force on Values and Ethics, Privy Council Office, 1996, Ottawa.

Federal Regulatory Process Management Standards: Compliance Guide, Treasury Board of Canada Secretariat, 1996, Ottawa.

Growth, Human Development, Social Cohesion, Draft Interim Report, Policy Research Committee, 4 October 1996, Ottawa.

Progress Report, Policy Research Committee, 1997, Ottawa.